How to read your DREAMS

CAVENDISH HOUSE

Credits

The Bodleian Library, Oxford p. 49.
Larry Burrows/Aspect p. 55. Roger
Charity p. 17. Salvador Dali/
A.D.A.G.P., Paris p. 60. John Fernley
pp. 25, 52. Fox-Rank p. 61. John
Garrett pp. 8, 16, 18, 26, 31. The
Mansell Collection pp. 52, 53. M.G.M./
C.I.C. p. 61. Oslo Kommunes
Kunstsamlinger p. 59. Popperfoto pp.
25, 52. F. Jurgen Rögner pp. 7, 12-13.
Sanders p. 33. Kim Sayer p. 63. John
Seymour p. 4. Trevor Sutton p. 6. The
Tate Gallery, London pp. 10, 21, 40.
Victoria and Albert Museum/Crown
Copyright p. 45. John Watney p. 43.
Chris Yates pp. 5, 15, 22, 29, 36, 39, 51,
57, 62, 64. ZEFA/Pictor Ltd p. 35.

Published by Marshall Cavendish Books Limited
58 Old Compton Street London W1V 5PA

© Marshall Cavendish Books Limited 1974, 1975, 1976, 1977, 1978,
1979, 1980, 1981,1982, 1983, 1984, 1985

Printed and bound by Grafiche Editoriali Padane S.p.A., Cremona, Italy

ISBN 0 85685 106 X

Introduction

Dreams have always fascinated man – ever since 5000 BC and before we have been delving into the world of sleep and trying to find answers or give meanings to the extraordinary visions which appear there. And now we know that exploring dreams can be positively helpful and rewarding. Most psychologists believe that your dreams can reveal the things which preoccupy your mind deep down, even if you don't recognize them immediately. Once you know what to look for, you will be amazed how much you can learn about yourself, your friends and family and, perhaps, how you can overcome the problems which are at the root of most dreams.

No matter how humdrum you feel life to be, if you look into your dreams you will find a whole new imaginative landscape that would be hard to think up during your waking hours.

Here is the background you will need to understand the importance of sleep and dreams, and how to extract the information from a puzzling jumble of dream pictures. Past ideas and future possibilities are all included, and there is a dossier of genuine dreams from all kinds of people for you to compare and contrast with your own personal dreamscape.

Contents

Dream
for
yourself

Most people think that dreams are some kind of night-time joke. How often has a friend come over at work or in the shops and said, 'I had the oddest, funniest dream last night'? This is usually the start of a good story, usually a jumble of strange ideas perhaps involving a mutual friend, set in the most unlikely circumstances or filled with such terror and fear that no one can understand the reason for it. The normal reaction is to marvel at the oddity of it all—and then forget about it. But you can get much more out of dreams than jokes or strange stories. It is interesting to note for instance that people always want to tell their dream

to someone, as if there is a natural desire to go back over the experience, to try and think it out. With a little knowledge and experience you'll be able to learn some valuable things about yourself and your friends— about character, aims, ambitions and the problems which are bothering your unconscious. You might even find a solution to a dilemma which has been worrying you for days.

The most important step is to realize that dreams are not disorganized nonsense. Your brain isn't resting by

Night-time experiences can seem as vivid as waking reality.

Dreams have their own logic – a car can be the driving force in your life; (right) falling can suggest a sense of losing a grip on life.

scrambling up thoughts and turning everything upside-down for a few hours while your body relaxes. Neither are dreams some frightening glimpse into the 'dark world' of the mind. There is nothing dangerous or harmful about dwelling on your dreams, though you don't need to be obsessive about it.

Psychology and dreams

Many people think that all the talk about 'the mind' and 'psychoanalysis' involved in dream interpretation is nonsense. But you should not make the mistake of thinking it is a pseudo-science, fit only for ridicule. The work of famous psychoanalysts like Freud and Jung has helped thousands of normal, healthy people, to say nothing of many cases of extreme mental disturbance. Their findings can be applied in a simple way to everyone's own experience of life. You don't have to be neurotic, obsessive or anything else so serious. Just as doctors can treat grave physical diseases but also show the world in general the basic rules of personal or home hygiene, so psychologists have shown well-balanced human beings how they can be more self-aware and lead, fuller happier lives.

What are dreams?

What are dreams exactly? There are many theories about the meaning of dreams but everyone basically agrees that they are a product of the unconscious mind. This is best explained by looking at what happens when people daydream. The mind is wide-awake and aware—that is, conscious. You might be going out shopping, knitting or filing cards in a perfectly ordinary way, but your thoughts wander on their own. Perhaps you go·over what happened last night, or more often, what you hope will happen in the future. Sometimes these daydreams become quite divorced from reality; people imagine themselves on Caribbean beaches or married to millionaires. While it lasts, a daydream seems vivid and true, but when you 'snap out of it' it is easy to forget. Something of the same process occurs in dreams which take place during sleep. The conscious, controlling part of the mind becomes relaxed (although it does not switch off all its powers) and a submerged layer of thoughts, ideas and feelings wells up. Because this part of the mind obeys its own logic, it describes things in its own direct way, using word-pictures and seemingly irrational chains of connections. This is why in dreams people do impossible things or shift quickly from scene to scene. The unconscious mind is going direct to the point without needing to progress in a logical sequence as the conscious mind does.

The other characteristic of dreams, which everyone who recalls them will recognize, is that they are often unusually vivid—either visually or in mood. Sometimes the feelings they generate can be so strong that they affect the dreamer's mood for the next day—sometimes called 'getting out of bed on the wrong side'. For instance, a successful businessman related a series of dreams he had during the early part of his career, all of which were set in a war situation. (War is one of the classic images of pressure or tension.) At first, while he was working on his own, his dreams involved his own attempts to avoid some nameless terror which came in a variety of guises. After he took control of a large department in a big company the war dreams continued, except his main preoccupation became trying to get the other people in the dream to cope with the attack, or whatever it happened to be. Significantly he could not recall the visual detail of the dreams—apart from the wartime setting—but the feelings of fear, panic and frustration associated with them re-mained particularly vivid.

On the good side, it is quite common to have a very happy or successful dream and to wake up feeling particularly pleased with yourself. Small children for example often dream of receiving gifts: they wake up feeling curiously elated and can be very down-hearted when they realize it was only a dream! Typical is the story of a small boy who was telling his mother in great excitement about his dream of the night before. He was being chased by a wolf and had tried to run into the house for protection through the kitchen door, but it would not open. He struggled and struggled as the fierce wolf drew nearer, then finally at the last minute, the door handle gave and he got inside to safety. The boy's mother replied in the usual way, 'Oh well, never mind, it was only a dream', to which the child retorted, 'Well, next time I have a dream, you leave the door open!' Children have to learn to distinguish between the 'inner space' of the unconscious and the 'outer space' of consciousness. Some primitive tribes still make no differentiation between the two.

This 'alternative reality' of dreams is very important. Allied to it is the fact that dreams happen entirely of their own accord, and we cannot make them happen or control their contents.

What dreams do

What are dreams for? Basically, they are the method by which the unconscious mind sifts and sorts experiences. If you can visualize the brain as an enormous receiving station, with all kinds of information going into it every day, then you will see that it has a large task to perform. During sleep, while the conscious part of the mind is inactive, the unconscious, (or subconscious) processes a vast jumble of material—new facts, situations, past experiences, unsolved worries, fears, desires and much more. It draws up emotions from the deepest recesses of the mind and memory and takes into account all the new information which the conscious mind has received. Then, in its own unique style, it presents a visual and emotional image to you—a dream. Perhaps you have a problem which you are consciously putting off because you do not wish to think about it. But it is still there and may well present itself to you in a dream. The sorting station is sending a message, 'Don't forget, don't overlook this'. Sometimes a dream will even offer a possible solution to such a problem.

As well as the unconscious, there is that deeper part already mentioned where the instincts, intuitions and emotions originate. These too are drawn up into dreams through the sorting house function, producing a very powerful effect on the mind. Just as people push problems to one side consciously, so also they ignore real feelings. It is interesting to note that people often say, 'What do you think about So-and-so, really, deep down?' or 'In my heart of hearts I believe such-and-such', as if in common speech they acknowledge the existence of this innermost part of the mind where strong, genuine feelings are to be found.

By recognizing where the material that goes into dreams comes from, you can begin to understand more of your true nature—your real views and attitudes, your feelings and needs, and by relating the dream-pictures to your everyday existence, get a better grip on your life-situation. Not all dreams are exactly problem-posers or -solvers, but they are a representation of some part of your life, often that part with which you cope least successfully.

> 'I dreamed I was dying in a lonely room. This funny doctor was there but no-one else. The doctor said there was nothing he could do but I was going to die. I wasn't in any pain — it wasn't a nightmare. I didn't really remember it until going to the office next morning. I kept thinking about it all day.'
> Businesswoman, 29

People who don't dream

What about people who say they never dream? If thinking about dreams is so helpful, why do some people never recall them—are they missing out in some way? Most of them are perfectly happy, average human beings, with no apparent disadvantage in comparison with those who seem to dream regularly. Laboratory experiments using the electro-encephalograph (EEG) machine to record brain 'waves' have revealed that people who do not recall their dreams have exactly the same trace patterns as those who remember their dreams vividly. In fact everyone dreams for regular periods during the night and people who think they never dream either forget them or have 'thoughts' in the night which they do not consider to be dreams—more like daydreams. If you are one of these 'non-recallers' try discussing dreams with people who do remember them. You will probably find that you begin to recall them more often.

What dreams can tell you

For those who can remember dreams, the next step is to uncover the real meaning behind them. The key to the subject is that dreams are what a famous American psychologist Calvin Hall once termed 'a letter to oneself'. Once you have learned to read this private letter, some fascinating home truths will emerge. Do not believe that dreams will necessarily show you the answers to all your problems—no dream ever repaired a damaged bank balance or turned an ugly duckling into a swan! But it might help you to see that money is not all-important and that a good face or figure is not the be-all and end-all of life.

The best way to start examining your dreams is simply to recall them during the following day. Just mulling them over, even if they seem quite non-sensical, will be of help. Sometimes a thought will suddenly spring into your mind as a result of these ponderings. It might appear at first to have no connection whatsoever with the dream, but a little more thought will reveal the link. For example, it often happens that a friend introduces you to someone about whom you have heard a great deal of praise and glory. You feel a small prick of doubt, but immediately dismiss it and try to socialize. In the end, you come to the conclusion that this new individual is 'not so bad' after all. It is possible that you will have a dream after such an encounter in which this charming and apparently successful person is turned into a ridiculous figure, a hideous monster or a creepy-crawly insect—depending on the nature of your real view. That first 'suppressed' reaction will come back in dream form, and conversely, dwelling on the dream could bring back the reaction.

Recording your dreams

Another way in which dreams can inform the dreamer is if they are studied over a period of time. Keep a notebook, writing down each dream either at night if you wake up from a particularly disturbing one (which will also help you to return to calm sleep) or first thing in the morning before getting up. Do not simply make a note of the basic situation of the dream—like 'Climbed mountain'—but try to catch in a word or two the essential feeling involved: 'Climbed mountain, made great effort, seemed to take a long time, but felt very pleased when top reached'. It is also very important to follow the sequence of events as they occur in the dream. You often find that you do things for reasons which, in waking life, you might think were totally

Below: Richard Hamilton's 'Interior II' conveys in pop art terms the theory that dream images are all reflections of the dreamer's personality. You can evaluate the significance of each image separately —combined together they will form a coherent expression of your inner state. The objects in this painting are familiar but fragmented;.in the same way, dream images are drawn from everyday objects but are presented in stark juxtaposition.

RICHARD HAMILTON/THE TATE GALLERY, LONDON

irrelevant or illogical. Next time you tell a dream to a friend note how often you say 'I did such-and-such *because*'. This feeling of compulsion is often very strong during dreams. Take the following example: 'I was running down a narrow dead-end street because a huge tank was bearing down on me.' The chain of events is part of the dream's private language—its message to you. Suppose the tank represents a person's sense of ambition. Perhaps the dream means that if the ambition is followed single-mindedly, without other possibilities being taken into account, it might be a mistake, for it will lead into a dead-end situation. The dream gives a clue to help you work out its contents by the order in which events are presented.

Dreaming in series

Similarly, series of dreams can be especially revealing. Although the dreamer may see himself very differently in each isolated dream, if they are put into a sequence, a pattern will emerge, revealing at least the area of his preoccupation.

Sometimes a series of dreams will show a progression in thinking. If you have some underlying conflict, such as an inability to get along with a relative, a series of dreams may play out numerous alternatives, like being very aggressive or being loving and submissive, or even murderous in hatred. What is difficult to recognize in one dream may be more easily seen when two or three dreams are put together to look for common features.

This serial aspect may seem difficult at first. Take the two dreams described here:

'I was going to a big, strange house in the country which my family had just moved into — but it was empty. I was being driven there in a car in my night clothes, all wrapped up in a blanket in the front passenger seat, but there was no one in the driver's seat. Suddenly I was there — I don't remember arriving — and I went up to a room where there was a man putting up wallpaper. It was incredible wallpaper, in three parts. The first part was a collage of sparkly Christmas cards. The second was a boat — a galleon made out of gold paper — and the third part had a Teddy bear stuck on to it. It was about 2 feet high, and in a running position, stuck on sideways. I was talking to

the decorator. I can't remember exactly what I said, but it was something about how much work must have gone into it, and the decorator was going on about how wonderful it was. Then suddenly I was dressed in my day clothes. Sue, a friend of mine, came in dressed in a funny coat and said, "Today's my day for learning". (I knew it was Tuesday, even outside my dream, and she goes to college on Tuesdays). Then I found a piece of paper which said "Please phone Clive before 19.19". Then the phone rang and I woke up and Clive was on the other end.'

'I was in this travelling show and there were many players but I was with the guy who owned the show and I looked like one of those "Barbie" dolls ... you know ... those "Cindy" dolls . . . and not looking at all human. I did all these astounding things which only a doll could do and which a human would hurt herself doing. At the end of the show I had a metal comb which I had to hold in my mouth and make it go round so it made my mouth bleed . . . the whole of the inside of my mouth was bleeding. I had to put my finger in my mouth and hold it up to the audience to show the blood to prove I was really human!'

There are certain elements common to both these dreams, even though at first glance they appear very different. For a start, there is a feeling of passivity around the dreamer in both cases: in the first dream she is being driven—as opposed to driving the car herself—and is all wrapped up, motionless, powerless, like a little child or baby. This ties in with the second dream's idea of being like a 'doll', that takes orders from a boss-man. Secondly, both dreams are connected with children. The doll is an object associated with childhood. In the first dream, the girl enters a room that sounds like a fantastic nursery, with pretty Christmas cards and Teddy Bear wallpaper. The dreamer herself could probably add greater meaning to this part of the dream by looking in her memory for incidents connected with boats, Teddy bears and Christmas. In general terms, these pictures suggest she is looking back into her childhood as a time when everything was done for her, with a 'lot of work going into it' as she says in the dream.

Obviously, connections with childhood

in the second dream are the doll, but in the main it is concerned with the present. The girl is on her own and somehow associated with a man who makes her do terrible tricks. It does not take a great deal of analytical skill to start wondering whether in real life this dreamer is mixed up with someone who is or has made her hide her real feelings and has hurt her. It might even be a more general situation: the girl might be afraid of having any relationship with a man at all. Only she can tell. Yet, even you as an outsider can progress quite far with this series of dreams. You can see clearly how the same problem-area is covered in both. Here is a girl, who remembers a comfortable happy time at home, now confronted with a new way of living and

relating to people, on her own and feeling apprehensive, even hurt, by her new experiences. The first dream moves on further from the happy childhood picture: there is another girl in it saying 'Today's my day for learning.' The message for the dreamer is 'Buck up and don't look back, let's get on with living, however difficult it is'. This links up quite specifically with the end of the other dream. The outside stimulus of the telephone ringing brings to mind the subject area of the problem, that is, dealing with men on an adult level. Comfortingly, the dream is urging her with a 'message' to make contact: 'Go on, give it a try'. The second dream about the doll sticks to the same situation but expresses the girl's fears about the possible outcome —being used and hurt. Incidentally, the dreamer was astonished at the accuracy of the insights in this inter-

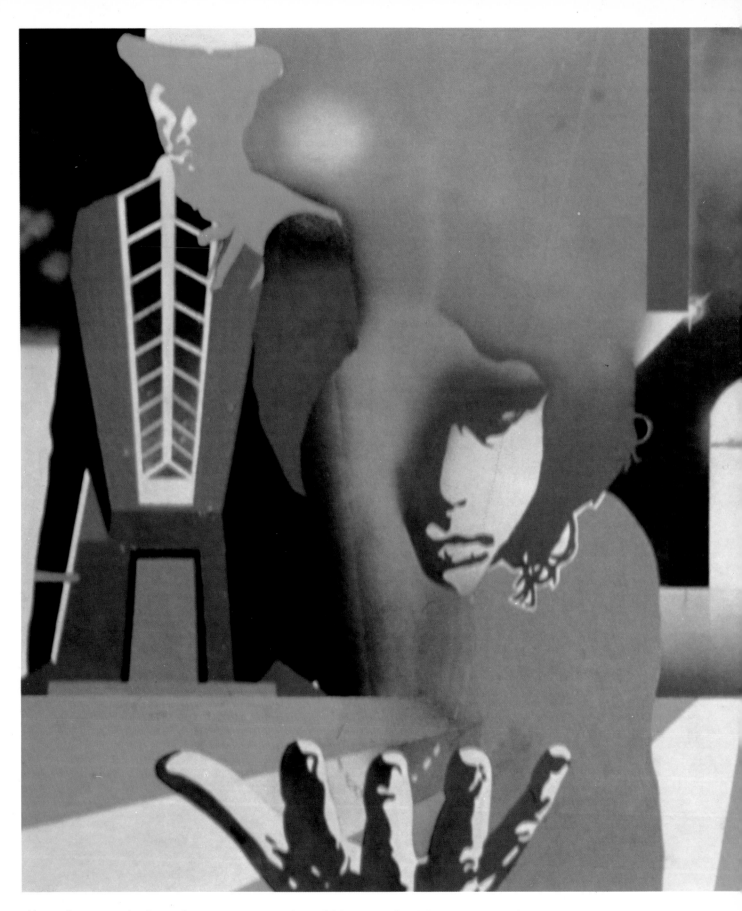

Above: Images can be drawn from any time in your past. They could be zebras from a childhood visit to the zoo combined with last week's holiday flight. These images in turn might be expressed in the style of some science fiction film you saw the evening before.

pretation, which was made without any background information.

No time in dreams

Another aspect of this link-up in dreams of different kinds of pictures is that the dreaming mind takes no notice whatsoever of time, which is part of the conscious mind's experience: it simply doesn't need it. In a dream, something that happened to you ten years ago may be relevant to something that is part of your life today. Look for

very helpful. To use the examples just discussed: if the girl's recollection of childhood was of a time when she was very unhappy and lonely, then obviously the dream would have a different message. The series might be saying 'You'll be hurt again just as you were before, so be careful'. Either way, the problem is a common one, that of reconciling the past with the present and growing up.

How to recall your dreams

For those people who seldom or never recall a dream and feel a little frustrated at the prospect of missing out in this personal 'fortune-telling', some comfort can be derived from the fact that telling yourself 'I'll have a dream tonight' can sometimes produce interesting results. Ann Faraday, a well-known British dream researcher, has formulated some rules to help people catch their dreams. She recommends setting an alarm clock to go off at two-hourly intervals from the usual falling-asleep time. In this way, you can be fairly sure of catching yourself during a dreaming patch. Even a once-nightly interruption will do, if the idea of more sounds like torture, but in this case, set the clock for much later in the night—between 3 and 5 am.

If you do wake up this way, it is essential to write the dream details down then and there or they will fade very quickly. Better still, use a cassette tape recorder if you have one, and keep it by the bedside. Failing that, tell it to your sleeping partner or say it out loud—this helps to get the details up into the conscious mind which then stores it in the recent memory.

At whatever time you awake with a dream whether in the night or in the morning, it is advisable to move slowly —do not jar yourself into reality if you want to catch the most details possible. Leaping out of bed to rush across the room for a pencil will probably result in your stopping dead in your tracks with a sudden blank in your mind. Move gently, slowly, into a sitting position— some people find it helpful to keep their eyes closed for a few moments while they capture as many details as they can. The small things in a dream can frequently be significant, as for example in making a serial record over a period of time. Perhaps a small detail in one dream may become the central part of another, or a picture with a similar connotation may appear subsequently. Either way, it is important to lose as little as possible so you can have plenty of material to ponder over.

common links in events, and do not concentrate on writing down only those dreams which seem to be the most coherent or the most like waking views of life.

It follows from this that if a picture or incident in a dream reminds you immediately of something in your past, you must note it down as well. Psychoanalysts have found that one of the most useful interpretations of a dream is that made by the patient himself. So even in studying your dreams in a non-clinical way, such connections will be

Analysis: nine dreams

If you could ask one hundred people what they thought was the mood conveyed in their dreams, about forty would probably answer that it was apprehension. About eighteen would say anger, then perhaps six would mention sadness. Only a lucky eighteen individuals would be able to state that happiness was the main emotional content of their dreams. The remaining eighteen would describe sensations of surprise, excitement or interest.

These figures were established in a very wide-reaching survey conducted in the early 1950s, just fifty years after the first publication of *The Interpretation of Dreams* by Sigmund Freud. In that space of time the issues he first investigated have been confirmed and modified. Nowadays we have a fairly clear picture of the sort of things people dream about. The following samples are typical of normal sleep experiences.

Sex on a desert island

Freud's great contribution to the understanding of dreams was his realization that they reflect unconscious thought processes, especially with regard to sexual drives. Sex can be presented directly, as in dreams which actually involve making love. More often the sexual message is hidden in some way. This is especially true where the dreamer has some sense of guilt or conflict between his desire and his conscience.

'I dreamt I was on a beautiful desert island, green parrots were flying overhead, and suddenly Marlon Brando appeared. I was wearing a very brightly patterned sarong thing, and he said I looked like a flower . . . the next thing we're sitting in a beautiful clearing in a thick shady forest, and there's a mass of fruit and food piled up for our picnic . . . the rest of the dream was all about . . . well, making love.'

The setting
This is a classic example of a sexual dream in more ways than the obvious ending. 'A beautiful desert island' is an exotic, faraway-from-it-all setting. Sex is often suggested in such lush or luxuriously different places. It is essential to notice the background setting of any dreams. Domestic, familiar places occur most frequently. Places of pleasure or sport, such as football grounds or swimming pools, are almost as common, whereas work places are much less frequent, in spite of the amount of time spent there in waking life.

The setting or background can reveal something about the meaning of a dream when evaluated in relation to the events taking place there. Here, clearly, the desert island reinforces the out-of-the-ordinary character of the dream and suggests that it is pure wish-fulfilment.

The hero
A glamorous film star like Marlon Brando may be part of the same desire for romance and sexual excitement. It is quite common to dream of famous people, colleagues from work or social acquaintances (like other people's husbands or wives) in this situation. It does not necessarily mean that you want to make love to that person in reality. You might simply be linking up a wish for sexual satisfaction with an example of the sort of person you like. Consider the character of the film star or friend in the dream, for it may give you some insight into the qualities you admire in a partner in real life. It is perfectly normal for a married person to dream about distant individuals in preference to real lovers or spouses. If your actual relationship is satisfactory then you will probably not reflect upon it often in a dream, which is usually a time for satisfying unmet desires or sorting out problem situations.

The role of the dreamer
In a dream such as this, you should also look at how you place yourself. Is the 'I' figure really like you? Do you find it laughable to think of yourself dressed in bright colours or hearing pretty compliments? Perhaps you think you are not very attractive or that your personality lacks real colour. Your dream may be compensating for these feelings. How do you respond to the idea of all that food? Do you eat it with appetite and pleasure or just toy with it? Remember that food is often a sexual symbol, representing the idea of appetite for sex as well as for sustenance. This is a good example of the way the sexual message of a dream can be hidden under another subject.

The great escape

According to Alfred Adler, another of the great dream psychologists, the commonest drive besides sex is that for power. Dreams frequently reveal the hidden desires of a personality or release some urges that do not find satisfaction in real life.

'I had a really vivid dream of being with a group of men, we were prisoners in a sort of castle — there were soldiers on guard duty everywhere. I organized the men into an escape group. I seemed to be able to speak several languages, so I was the leader, and we dug a tunnel to get out. Then we were climbing over a very high wall . . . it seemed to take ages. Lastly I remember standing on an open train carriage, and rushing through countryside, feeling excited we'd escaped, but worried in case we were being followed.'

You might have guessed already that this is a man's dream—not that women do not also dream of action and power, but proportionately more men than women are concerned with these issues in dreams. This is a reflection of the differences in physical characteristics and the roles usually assigned to the two sexes in society.

The role of the dreamer
Here, the 'I' in the dream is significant again. Is the dreamer rather timid in real life, working at a job that lacks any outgoing action? If this were true, then the dream would be compensatory—making up for the lack he feels in his situation. It might also be an expression

Right: Doorways, staircases, castles, churches—however remote from everyday experience—are common dream images because of their general emotive value.

*Jungians believe that everything in a
dream is a reflection of some part of
yourself, so being alone in a bare room
might suggest a need to look inward.
A Freudian interpretation might give
this image a sexual connotation.*

of a man's need to dominate, to organize, to be brave and tough. Alfred Adler, who started out as a disciple of Freud but subsequently developed his own views, placed a lot of emphasis on this aggressive drive in people, believing it was as important as sex.

The influence of recent experience
Such a dream might be prompted by watching a Western or wartime adventure at the movies or on television. However, it is important not to overestimate the 'trigger' of a dream as its cause. The recent experience might produce the particular situation of the dream, but it has nothing more to do with why that particular event—of all others in the recent past—should be retained and re-created in the dream.

Private doubts and fears
A very large proportion of dreams dwell on feelings of doubt, fear or inadequacy. There is a trace of that in this dream, for the escaped man is still worried that he is being followed. In other words, even after he has shown himself to be brave and resourceful, he thinks that it is still not enough and he hurries away on the train to the next challenge. This dreamer probably pushes himself too hard and should learn to accept his limitations. He might not appear like this at all in real life. It is surprising what doubts are expressed in this private way.

Black cats in the basement

'I went into a tall house, down a dark staircase. I don't know why I was there but I seemed to know which way to go. I got into a dark room, it seemed empty, then suddenly I realized it was seething with cats. Black cats. Then I realized that I had a baby in a kind of papoose, strapped to my back. I turned to get out of the room, and a cat jumped on my back and was clinging on to the baby. I tried to get out of the house and was running along trying to get the cat off my back all the time.'

Animals and instincts
Such a dream leads inevitably to an analysis of images and symbols in dreams. What do the pictures suggest to the dreamer? There are two main levels of interpretation here. Take the cats first. By and large animals represent the instincts, the emotional, intuitive parts of a person's nature as opposed to the rational, controlling parts. But it is also significant to find out what the dreamer actually thinks of the animals in her dream, in this case black cats. If for example the person had a favourite pet that died, there might be a strong sense of loving and deep loss associated with cats in her mind. By contrast, the girl who related this dream had always rather disliked them. Their feline movements were too 'creepy-crawly' for her, and she did not like the suddenness with which they bare their claws. This relates back to the general symbolic values associated with them: intuitive, instinctive, especially female emotions. Notice how this is linked in the dream with the picture of the baby tied to the girl's back. A fear of her own feelings is being expressed.

The setting
The setting of the dream as always yields some meaning too. Houses occur frequently in dreams. Living rooms, bedrooms and kitchens turn up most, in that order. Basements and cellars are places where 'base' deeds are committed, where deep feelings are allowed out. The dream seems to suggest not only a fear of discovering deep-hidden feelings, but a hint of the anxiety or hurt that could result from giving way to them.

Different parts of the whole
It is worthwhile analyzing a dream as if everything in it, including people, is a part of the dreamer.
This house stands for the girl herself: the cellar, her own instinctive feelings; the baby may not mean another human being or a desire for children, but a part of the girl herself that she is afraid to express. She is afraid of getting hurt if she does. Obviously, the dreamer herself can tell best to what the images refer. This dream does not answer the questions, but poses them. Somewhere in her unconscious there are deep feelings trying to be expressed.

The turquoise pool

Other dreams work through a problem to a solution. Most of us have had a dream at some point which is repeated, perhaps even over a span of several years. These are known as 'recurring' dreams. Quite often they relate back to some incident in childhood, if you think

The cat is a familiar image of mystery, associated with magic or religion. In general terms, it represents the intuitive, instinctive, feminine qualities.

closely about it. These dreams are often nightmares and it is the old, familiar quality of only half understanding that is especially frightening.

'I dreamt I fell into a lovely turquoise pool — a beautiful blue, with sponges and ferns floating in the water, growing down the sides of the rocks. At first it looked very pretty and I swam about. Then I realized that it was getting darker, deeper, and I was going down . . . I couldn't breathe, I struggled to come up, and I woke up trying to gasp and take in air.'

Re-living the birth trauma
The endurance of an experience from childhood or birth is partly due to the extreme vividness of the incident in a child's mind and partly results from any reinforcement in later life. This dream is typical of 'drowning' dreams which have been explained by Freud as a lingering remembrance of the birth experience or 'trauma', the uterine waters and the journey from the womb, just as he interpreted 'flying' dreams as a manifestation of sexual ecstacy. If later life brings a sense of insecurity and fear to add to the original experience, then a fear-expressing dream on the same theme may result.

Resolving childhood experiences
Sometimes nightmares refer not to birth experiences but to some childhood incident not resolved or coped with at the time. Even a memory of learning to swim or slipping in the bath might be so vivid that a repeating nightmare remains. Dreams can then be helpful: they go over an incident many times but modify the experience until the difficulty is resolved.

In this case, a child had been playing near a pool and had overheard someone remark on its depth. Her dream was a realization of what might have happened if she had slipped—acting as a very vivid warning.

The collective unconscious
Another theory from the great psychologist and theoretician Carl Gustav Jung suggests that monsters in dreams or other terrifying experiences in nightmares are part of our 'collective unconscious'—a sense of shared experience accumulated over thousands of years of evolution in the unconscious minds of all human beings. These experiences manifest themselves in dreams, always in repeated, 'archetypal' ways. Drowning in seas, oceans or lakes is one such motif. (This difficult concept is de-scribed fully in the section on Jung's theories.)

A legal salad dressing
On the brighter side, a number of delightful dreams seem to satisfy our wildest hopes in improbable ways. Children especially dream in these wish-fulfilling ways because in real life they have little power to do things for themselves. This idea of wish-fulfilment is central to dream interpretation.

'I dreamed I was looking for a job with a firm of lawyers, and I went for an interview to a place. When I got in, one of the partners was mixing up a lovely salad dressing, another was carefully warming glasses for drinks over a roaring fire. The secretary was sorting out beautiful new books — pretty books on all the things I like — crafts, biographies and so on, and putting them on the shelves. I said to myself, "I hope they take me on here, it looks like a good place to work". I felt very happy and decided about it.'

The value of images
Here is a clear case of wishful dreaming, for the girl involved was in real life looking for a job at the time. Why does the dream translate it into such unlikely, incongruous terms? It shows the value of the images of a dream, for all these things—cooking, drinking, reading—are the things that give the dreamer pleasure. Putting them all in one place is like saying 'It's got everything to make me happy'. It could also define a conflict between the job hunting and domestic life. The dreamer, a woman, might secretly be wondering whether she would be better off staying at home. However, the domestic details are highly idealized, with roaring fires and cosy drinks. It suggests that the first analysis is appropriate, merely bringing together images of happiness.

Following the plot
Always follow the sequence of events in a dream: here the conclusion is very significant, for there is a definite decision that getting a good job would be very nice. The dreamer expresses her aim, after a possible conflict.

Parents in the pavilion
Contrasts or comparison between two possible lines of action is the major area of dream experiences. The one above shows a typical problem for a woman, the choice of taking a job or taking care of her home. Even more fundamental to both sexes is the battle between the desire for freedom and the need for security, especially when growing up and leaving home.

'I'd just got married to someone who in real life is a friend I've known a long time and I'm very close to, but my parents have never met him. The two of us were standing in a huge playing field, like a football ground, and 'way, 'way in the distance inside the pavilion my parents were standing with the rest of my family. We were just about to go off when my parents called, "Haven't you forgotten something?" I thought, "No, I don't think so, I've got enough money etc." They called again, "Haven't you forgotten something?" and again I couldn't think of anything else I needed. They called again, so eventually I relented and we went back all the way over this field to the pavilion where they were standing. When we got there, they said, "We haven't been introduced", so I introduced my "husband" to them and we went off.'

Dreaming about marriage
It is surprising but true that when girls dream about marriage they often put someone they would not expect to marry in the role of bridegroom. This seems to express the general importance and apprehension that women attach to marriage. Men much more normally dream of marriage to girls they do intend to marry in reality. The conflicts inherent in marriage do not seem to strike them to the same degree.

The setting
The choice between family ties and starting a life with a man of her own is expressed here in the image of the football field. The step she had taken means standing out alone in the 'playing field' of life. An element of competition, or striving in the face of the crowd, is suggested. In the pavilion everything is snug and friendly. There is the companionship of the family to be enjoyed. Also, pavilions are places where people relax from the rigours of the game. No one has to bother about the rules of the field.

The spoken words
So in the dream, the conflict is stated and the choice is made, but the dreamer is still not sure. 'Have you forgotten

something?' her parents call. The dreamer could be expressing guilt that she has broken her family ties rather sharply and ought to keep in touch more often. It could be that she still feels that she has to be 'sent off' by her parents, just as a little girl gets dispatched to a party: 'Make sure you're good: have you got a clean handkerchief?' It seems to be that sort of question here. Finally, the dreamer relents and goes back—after the mystical 'three calls', a detail which Jung, with his insistence on religious and folkloric elements would have found very important. The girl makes the introduction—that is, makes the link between her new life and her past—and then goes off.

Problems and solutions

This is a very clear demonstration of the way that dreams not only present a problem or a conflict, but frequently come up with some suggestion for a solution. In real life this girl would probably feel much better about her independence if she matched it with a family contact. It could be that she has always fought hard to stand on her own two feet, whereas in reality she now lacks a little of the kindly assurance that good family ties can give. As with all dream analysis, it is the dreamer herself who must sift the likely explanations and accept the correct, meaningful one.

The woman on the cliff

Perhaps less commonly identified are those dreams which not only offer a solution, but positively inspire the dreamer. Most famous people whose lives have called for tremendous courage in adversity or for a particularly strong sense of ambition can recall dreams where their goal was presented to them in some uplifting way. On a more personal level, we can dream about our better natures, pulling through or surviving a difficult time in life. Jung developed a theory that certain male or female figures in dreams are not necessarily sexual partners, but representatives of the 'opposites' in each person. For a woman, this is her Animus, or male counterpart; for a man, his Anima. These figures can appear in inspirational or guiding roles.

'This dream I had about 12 or 13 years ago but I remember it clearly, it was so vivid. I was in a car being driven along — I was in the passenger seat but I never saw the driver full face, only in profile. We were driving along a coast road with the sea on my side and fields on the driver's side running right down the road with no fence or ditch. The grass was incredibly green. After a while the road began to climb steeply up a cliff, and there was a sheer drop now on my side. On and on, up and up we drove until suddenly the road stopped at the bottom of a sheer crag. At the top stood three figures in dark clothes — two men with a woman between them. I didn't recognize her, though she seemed familiar. I got out of the car to take a closer look. The driver remained seated. I couldn't see any way of getting up the cliff, but then the woman, who was quite good-looking and well-spoken, said to me, "It's not as difficult as it looks. I for one would be most disappointed if you didn't make the effort". Then I started to climb the cliff-face up to her and to my surprise found it wasn't too difficult; as I went, I found handholds and footholds. As I got to the top, the woman leaned down and gave me her hand, helping me up. Then I woke up.'

The search for a goal

This man's dream is disturbingly vivid in its sense of striving and searching for a goal. Hopefully, the dreamer derived some comfort from this vision of a way out of his problems, which in his real life were causing him a great deal of unhappiness.

The car

First, the image of the car stands for a 'journey through life' that contains strongly mechanical or dissatisfying elements. Compare this with dreaming of riding a horse, a natural and exciting method of transport. The suggestion is reinforced by the fact that the dreamer is a passenger, carried through life by a person he doesn't really see properly. Remember that all parts of a dream may be analyzed as reflections of the dreamer himself: this driver is the 'front man' of the dreamer's own personality, not really matching up to his own true sense of himself, but somehow going through the motions of living.

The setting

Dreams are remarkably accurate in the location of an event. Here, the dreamer has the sea on his side. The sea is a symbol of the unconscious, creative forces of the universe and of the 'psyche', or mind. This is the potential area of the man's mind, whereas on his driver's side, there is green grass. You might overlook such a very familiar connection in your own dreams—this image suggests the common phrase 'the grass is always greener on the other side'. Is this the way of life that the dreamer really wants? Is it perhaps just a general discontent that things should be better, more interesting or exciting?

'I went into my parents' house while they were away. I'd just got in through the front door when I sensed that there was someone else in the house. I saw an ultra-enormous man standing in the kitchen with his back to me, sorting through the drawer where all the kitchen knives are kept. I tried to shout but no words came out and I then swivelled round and tried to run out of the house but my feet were completely glued to the floor. I looked over my shoulder to see if he really was still there and saw that he was about to turn round and see me. I then passed out!'
Fashion journalist, 22, female

The climb

The steep climb is a widely-found way of expressing a problem, a difficulty encountered in life. Unfortunately for this man, the endless struggle just leads to more difficulty, until part of him thinks 'I can't go on like this.' This is symbolized by the end of the road at the bottom of the crag.

The three figures

But there are figures at the top of the cliff—the two sides of himself and a kindly encouraging woman, who represents his Anima. For the first time in the dream, the man does something positive. He gets out of the car, leaving his driver behind. The inspirational force leads him to face the challenge of

William Blake's 'Ascent of the Mountain of Purgatory' combines three major dream symbols. The ocean represents the unconscious, the untapped source of creative potential; the climb of the mountain suggests the upward struggle through life, the vision of the woman, a perfect example of the Anima, stands for the inspiration and encouragement to carry on.

Canto 4

his problems and to surmount them. There are footholds in the cliff, just as there are remedies for life's crises.

The will to survive
This dream is a wonderful expression of a man's unconscious will to survive against the odds, to search out his true identity and make a better life for himself. No one can doubt the sincerity of his inner voice, which in a moment of weakness will not permit him to give up. It is not surprising that this man still remembers his moment of truth over a decade later.

A tractor in the living room

The sense of urgency that imbues many dreams demonstrates the power of the mind to force messages up from the unconscious to the surface. Fears, desires, drives or hopes can be expressed in this dream language. Dreams seem to draw our attention to problems or facts consciously overlooked.

'In my dream the living room in my house was extended into a long hall, like a room in a stately palace. The same carpet I've got in real life was laid all down the length of it. What was silly was that some idiot had driven a huge tractor or tank right down this hall and made two great torn-up track marks all down the carpet. A man was lurking about at the end of the room, and I spent most of the dream calling out indignantly, "Who the hell did this?" and trying to get the man to apologize.'

The immediate problem
This dream deals with a most immediate problem. The woman who related it had been dressmaking the night before while watching television and, rather than stand in a cold kitchen, had ironed a few pattern pieces on the floor over a towel. The next day she recalled the dream, but couldn't think what it meant at all. Then, later that same afternoon, her husband noticed a six-inch long stain on the living room carpet. It proved to be a scorch mark where the hot iron had accidentally gone off the towel on to the floor the night before. The woman had not noticed this at all at the time—in fact, it took some minutes for her to realize

Many people have recurrent dreams of their ideal landscape, possibly recalling a happy incident in the past. Distortion of size is often characteristic of childhood memories.

how the mark had been made. Somehow, the incident had registered in her unconscious mind, and her dream had tried to bring it to her attention.

The missing marquee

Dreams can range from the sublime to the ridiculous in their content and intention, as these last two analyses show. A general principle seems to be that dreams very rarely deal with outside, important events in the world, but only with those that have a strong emotional value to the dreamer. Even wars only come up as expressions of man's aggressive tendencies.
The vast storehouse of the unconscious turns newly received information into a message of personal value. Just as we are serious one minute and silly the next, so our dreams reflect the gamut of human experiences. Take this example of a nationally significant event:

'I was invited to a reception at the home of Mr and Mrs Peter Phillips, parents-in-law of Princess Anne. When I got there, the place seemed very small: a thatched cottage of smaller-than-life size, with a large expanse of green grass in front. I went up to the door where Mr Phillips stood waiting to receive me. "Where's the marquee for the ball?" I asked. He laughed and said, "Oh, we're not having one, the party's out at the back." People seemed to be going through the house, but I turned into a room sort of tacked on to the side of the building. It turned out to be a very pretty, attractive child's bedroom with flowery wallpaper. A boy aged about twelve was asleep in bed. Somehow I knew it was Mark Phillips' younger brother, (although I know he hasn't really got one), but at the same time it was my own son. I was pleased about this, because it meant that I could check if he was all right, tuck him in and give him a cuddle.'

Scaling things down
This dream shows just how much more interesting than fact or fiction your dreams can be. The most obvious explanation is that the dreamer had been watching the wedding of Britain's Princess Anne on television the day before. This is reflected in the detail that some things seemed smaller than reality, like watching a little screen. The transformation into a cottage and the homelike detail 'It's out at the back'

brings the occasion down to a more immediate scale of values—a good example of the unconscious feeling that importance in social, public terms has little to do with genuine experiences of living. Incidentally, it echoes a happening in the dreamer's own life, for extensive building alterations were taking place at the back of her own house.

Motherly love
The final part of the dream is a picturesque and sincere expression of maternal care and affection. In the midst of this personally exciting occasion, the mother thinks of her child. It may seem unlikely, but puns in dreams are very common, and the whole association of royalty, and the 'marquee' bring to mind the picture of a little prince, (in French, *marquis*). It is a nice way of referring to one's offspring!

The bedroom
There may be more than sweetness and light in this apparently loving dream. Is there any significance in the situation of the bedroom just 'tacked on' to the house? It could be an expression of worry or doubt about the dreamer's way of combining her roles as a socially interested person and a dutiful mother. The dream gets round the problem by having a party and putting the child in the next room. Thus, any guilt feelings are overcome.

Looking for the answers

These dream samples demonstrate the enormous variety and depth of meaning that you can find in a superficially nonsensical experience. All the analyses show you how to progress, step by step, through the various stages of the dream. Clearly it is best to start your own efforts by contemplating complete dreams if you can.
Fragmentary recollections are more puzzling at first, but if all you have is 'snatches', then try to keep a record of them over days or weeks and then approach them with the same lines of thought shown here. The individual theories and meanings are described in depth in the sections following. You should always consider the pros and cons in your analysis. Do not write off a dream in one dimension, that is, 'Oh, this is pure wish-fulfilment/expression of fear/sexual fantasy/compensation/ etc . . .' Try to mull over all possible explanations. If you grow accustomed to this habit, then your final choice of an interpretation is more likely to be accurate, helpful and revealing.

Psychology and dreams: the theories

The pictures and stories presented to us in sleep are so strange and varied that it is not surprising to find so many different theories about their meaning. These range from the pure fantastical to the downright mechanical, comparing the mind to a machine.

The main reason for looking at the more important of these theories is that it helps to put your own ideas into perspective. Your interpretation will be more successful because you will have a solid background from which to work. You will be able to consider all the major factors that have been discovered about the world of dreams and to apply them to your own experiences.

Freud—the great innovator

One of the first great contributions to the study of dreams was made by Sigmund Freud. For many people he symbolizes the psychiatrist, the 'head-shrinker', more than any of the other famous names.

One possible explanation for this is the emphasis he laid on sex. All the cartoons showing patients lying on couches and doctors with notepads saying 'Tell me about your childhood' are based upon the Freudian view of psychoanalysis. He believed that everyone is born with basic urges which are suppressed as we grow up and learn to conform to society. So it can be helpful to go back and find out exactly when a certain urge was first curbed in childhood.

Perhaps some of Freud's ideas are laughable today—in stating his views, he had to exaggerate them; otherwise, no one would have paid any attention. If his theory about dreams seems 'sex-mad', consider that in a recent survey, 85% of the men admitted they had sexual dreams and 72% of the women agreed. It is the commonest of all dream subjects—and after all in real life, a good sexual relationship is one of the major reasons for a person's happiness and peace of mind.

What exactly did Freud believe? First, that all dreams are 'wish-fulfilling' of the sexual or aggressive impulses in human nature. These urges are with you from birth, but social training keeps them under control. Obviously,

to live in an ordered society you cannot go around gratifying your basic urges all the time.

Only in dreams, when your conscious mind is not on top of the situation, can these suppressed urges have a chance to come out. Freud believed this and explained why we dream in a different 'language'; not like real life, but doing absurd things with no clear sense of logic as we usually know it.

Because these urges are totally controlled by the conscious part of the mind, it is as if they can only be allowed out at night 'in disguise', using strange combinations of events and a secret sign language to get past the 'guard'— the conscious mind on patrol.

> 'There was a couple that I was watching. They were almost in silhouette. The girl was sitting semi-crossed legged, and the guy was sitting next to her and they were both naked. He just leaned round and touched her on the side of her hip, and she let out this incredibly sort of ecstatic sigh. Every time he touched her, she just went into an incredible convulsion and she started really arching her back. Then her legs came round and she just put her arm round him . . . it was very sensuous. Then she came round on top of him.'
> Motor mechanic, male, 22

The sexual sign language

Even if dreams do not appear to be about sex at all, Freud maintained that under the surface they invariably are. If a dream merely seems to pick out an event from yesterday or a recollection from the past, Freud thought that the incident was chosen out of all other possibilities because it linked up specifically with the urge being expressed in the dream.

Freud's list of sexual sign language seems endless: in the attempt to disguise the true nature of the dream, the unconscious uses a wide variety of

normal everyday objects to stand for sexual things: 'All elongated objects, such as sticks, tree trunks and umbrellas, may stand for the male organ, as well as long sharp weapons, such as knives, daggers and pikes. Boxes, cases, chests, cupboards and ovens represent the uterus and also hollow objects, ships and vessels of all kinds. Rooms in dreams are usually women.' With this means of disguise, the conscious is not alarmed and so allows us to sleep on peacefully. The 'watchful' part of the mind does not see through to the basic urge that is being expressed in a wish-fulfilling dream.

This theory may at first seem ridiculous but if someone has a sexual problem, it is more than likely that Freud's method will help to interpret their dream world. A young girl at college, worried about finding a boy-friend yet unsure of her ability to cope with sex, dreams of a large black gun firing off into a bare white room. There can hardly be the need for a psychoanalyst to help her see the wish-fulfilment suggested by that dream!

The sexual urge is very often expressed through other basic desires, like the appetite for food. Anyone watching the scene in the film *Tom Jones* in which the hero enjoys a frankly flirtatious meal with a loose lady must admit that their smacking of lips over the roast chicken hints at more than stomach hunger. In a dream, enjoying a meal with gusto can stand for an open, eager attitude towards satisfying sexual desires. A common type of man's dream goes like this:

> 'I walk into a beautiful dining chamber with glowing lights and a magnificent feast spread out on the table in the centre. Other people seem to be helping themselves freely to the food and wine, enjoying it all enormously. I want to go and help myself but cannot move forward. Finally a beautiful girl comes over and gives me a plate of food. I accept but, when I eat it, it tastes like liver and makes me feel sick.'

According to Freud, this dream represents a man's fear of sex—his inability

Sigmund Freud (1856-1939), born in Moravia, moved to Vienna at the age of four. His first passion was science, but he made medicine his career and explored the treatment of mental disorders. He dealt with people suffering from hysteria and soon developed the idea that by bringing to the surface the original reason or experience that caused a condition, the patient could be cured. This 'psychocatharsis' (*catharsis*: Greek for purging or cleansing) expanded into the field known as depth psychology or psychoanalysis.

He believed that the unconscious mind exerts a powerful influence over the conscious one and that fundamental instinctive urges are often coped with by pushing them out of sight or making them more socially acceptable by the process of 'sublimation'. More startling was his idea of 'infantile sexuality'; that is, from birth we experience sexual urges, at first directed solely towards the mother, who supports life.

His key work, *The Interpretation of Dreams* (1900), sets out his basic theories. Unlike Jung, Freud always maintained an 'analytical', scientific approach to the human personality, reducing problems to causes, which he saw sexually. This 'reductive' approach reduces the patient's present situation to its component parts through deep analysis of his past experiences.

Towards the end of his life, Freud gained wide recognition, especially in America. Because he was Jewish, Freud fled the Nazis in 1938. He settled in England and died the following year in London.

Alfred Adler (1870-1937) was born in Vienna, Austria, and after studying medicine became a disciple of Sigmund Freud. He defended Freud's views vigorously in the early days of their friendship but after nine years, his own ideas diverged from Freud's emphasis on the sexual urge underlying man's behaviour, and he set up an independent school of thought. Adler developed 'Individual Psychology', the study of people as goal-oriented individuals seeking personal perfection and wholeness.

His most significant theory was that everyone has difficulty in relating his own self-centred satisfaction and happiness to a contentment derived from fitting in to a group or society and his idea of 'will-to-power' led to wide acceptance of the 'superiority' and 'inferiority' complexes. Through dreams, Adler felt a person could better understand his aggressive impulses and desire for fulfilment. He sees what he really thinks of himself. The aim of Adlerian psychology is to help people fit their view of themselves into an acceptable social form. His studies were mainly concerned with the misfits of the world—criminals, drug-takers, drop-outs. He wanted to help people fit in. Freud and Jung were concerned with freeing the 'real' person inside and gave no emphasis to the world that this newly emerged self would find around him.

Adler achieved widespread recognition in his later years. He taught at Columbia University in New York City and at the Long Island College of Medicine, New York. He died on a lecture tour, in Scotland, in 1937.

Carl Gustav Jung (1875-1961) was a Swiss psychologist and psychiatrist. After studying in Basel and Paris, he became a disciple and friend of Sigmund Freud, the foremost psychologist of the time. After a few years, however, Jung developed a separate view and in 1914 formally broke away from Freud and his views. Jung took a much more religious, philosophical and mystical approach to the human personality than Freud's more scientific method, which delved into the root causes of problems.

Among Jung's contributions to the field of psychology was his explanation of the personality, or psyche, in terms of three systems that interact with each other. These are the conscious, the unconscious, and the 'collective unconscious'. The last was of great importance in explaining the meaning of dreams, for Jung was able to show that all people in the world show certain basic, inherited ideas, experiences or concepts expressed in eternal themes. These he called 'archetypes'. Jung was especially interested in mythology, alchemy, and world religions. During the 'thirties and 'forties he made various trips to Africa, Mexico, North America and the Far East to gather information and inspiration for his numerous books and essays.

Jung survived two world wars—he actually forecast the coming of the first in a vivid dream—and died in his homeland at Zurich in 1961.

Dreams can express repressed sexual fantasies and unconscious aggressive desires.

to find a happy sexual relationship. The fact that he sees everyone else around him enjoying it only makes him more inadequate and unable to cope. Interestingly the girl takes the first step, by giving him the plate of food (that is, making an advance). In real life, this man probably worries about girls a great deal, thinking they are a bit

> 'I am standing on a bank on
> the edge of water, but it
> isn't really water. I'm
> standing with my mother, my
> sister and my cousin. Then I
> dive in and as I dive in I
> look down my body and I've
> changed. I am now a girl
> with a female body in a black
> bikini. Then I hit the
> water and I come up and now
> I'm back to me again as a guy.
> I look up to the bank
> and everyone has blank faces
> and there are all sorts of
> breakers, breakers across the
> water. There are breakers
> all across the beach . . . like
> a beach I used to go to when
> I was a kid.
> I start walking down . . . but it
> carries on and gets a bit
> vaguer . . . it's no longer water,
> but in a building and I walk
> down into a room and then it
> becomes an old concert we had
> when we were at art college
> and I am in the cloakroom with
> Andy Fraser and people from
> the pop group Free. It's really
> weird. I recognize the room,
> but it's not the same and we
> are all standing there going,
> "Oh it's no good, it's not like
> it used to be".'
> Student, 20, male

'forward'. To tie in with Freud's view that personal recollection may support the sexual nature of a dream, it might turn out that the young man was often given liver as a child: his mother would say 'It's good for you, eat it up'. This would suggest a confused attitude about women, that he has not grown up sufficiently to be on his own feet and out of his mother's influence. (Freud believed that sexual feelings start with a child's desire for the mother in boys and the father in girls.) Perhaps the dream is also expressing the man's fear that if he does give way to his sexual urges, punishment will result as it did when he was a child.
Nowadays, people have a much broader

view of sex and the Freudian view seems a bit one-sided at first. But in his lifetime during the late 19th century, young people (especially women) were brought up to regard sexual feelings or any other impulsive, natural outburst of emotion as socially forbidden. The upper middle classes of Vienna, where he lived and worked, were particularly straight-laced and admiring of controlled intellectual pursuits. No one spoke about feelings or passions and they were only given way to in deep secret, in the boudoirs and brothels inhabited by 'fallen' women. No wonder that most of Freud's patients were more confused and anxious about sexual feelings than anything else. His thoughts were naturally concentrated on this area and this is reflected in his findings.

A main difficulty with Freud's theory is that not all dreams are concerned with wish fulfilment. Later in his life, Freud too began to change his mind about this part of his work. Take the example given above: Freud's earlier interpretation would be more appropriate if the man in the dream took the plate of food from the girl, gobbled it all up, and asked her for more! The bad endings are explained by saying that the conscious mind on patrol is sufficiently alerted to these feelings coming out that it steps in and puts everything in order once again. It adds on the 'right' ending to crush the urge once more. In this way, Freud managed to keep up his theory that all dreams do express the wish-fulfilment of a basic sexual or aggressive desire.

The influence of Freud

Much of what Freud uncovered in his study of dreams has passed into our everyday life. A large proportion of film or television advertising is based on the wish-fulfilment principle. Just like a dream, the cigarette or alcohol promoter says, 'Here is an ideal world—fulfil your urge to be a sex king or goddess of love by using our product'. If you want some practice at recognizing objects with a Freudian sexual link, try studying the advertisements. Long sleek cars, full of power, that 'respond' to every command; 'satisfying' cigarettes, smoked by two in a field of corn; 'long cool drinks' in exotic places, followed by high dives into deep blue seas —the underlying sexual tone soon becomes very evident. What about those after-shave lotions that have women falling at the feet of judo champions? In these pictures, sex and aggression are very directly combined.

Letting off steam in dreams

Aggression is not necessarily the desire to go out and fight with guns or boxing gloves. In a much wider sense it means the basic drive for power or domination. Alfred Adler, one of Freud's best-known followers, expanded this view. He put forward the idea that everyone has an equally strong drive within them —the need to dominate. Furthermore, this usually springs from some basic inadequacy or lack which is subconsciously recognized at an early age. The rest of life is spent trying to compensate for it. Adler's theory has been popularized in such ideas as small men like Napoleon lusting for power or that bald men are very sexual to make up for their supposed lack of looks.

It may seem that both Freud and Adler take a fairly dim view of human nature. Their ideas are based on a sort of unending warfare between basic drives and the need to keep them under control. Letting these drives out in wish-fulfilling or power satisfying dreams is like letting the steam out of a kettle: if they are permanently bottled up, a severe nervous breakdown could result. So dreams provide a convenient escape valve.

This does not explain why many people actually wake up from their dreams. If the Freudian view was entirely right, then everyone would always sleep peacefully after a dream, having worked off some infantile wish or urge. But quite often the reverse occurs and we are very disturbed by the things that take place during dreams. It seems sometimes that a dream is acting as a voice of conscience, especially in terrifying dreams or nightmares.

Jung versus Freud

Carl Gustav Jung disagreed quite forcibly with Freud and his followers over this idea of dreams, as well as the view that repressed sexual or domination drives are the key to understanding the sign language of dreams. Jung saw clearly that Freud's great achievement was in drawing people's attention to the idea of the unconscious mind and how he related it to dreams. But he disagreed with Freud on a number of fundamental points. For one thing, Freud always used dreams as a way of getting back to the basic cause of a problem. Usually he found it in some important event in childhood—even in the moment of birth—which had affected the patient's view of himself throughout his life. Freud believed that unearthing the problem through psy-

choanalysis, including a discussion of a person's dreams, could often lead to a cure. Once the basic urge is recognized and coped with in real life, the obsession or fear produced by keeping it forcibly locked up inside would disappear.

For example, Freud describes a young man he once helped who had a morbid fear of going out in the street because he thought he would kill everyone in sight. It gradually emerged from his dreams and remembrances of childhood that he had at one stage heartily disliked his father, so much so that at the age of seven he had made a feeble but deeply-felt attempt to kill him. When his father eventually died the young man felt

very guilty, or rather felt that he should. He transferred his feeling to everyone outside and punished himself by locking himself up in his room all day. Once he recognized the urge dating back to early childhood, he was able to come to terms with his fear and greatly improved.

Jung however, took an entirely different view of dreams. He admitted that a great deal of what Freud had discovered was true, but he believed that the language of dreams was not just some secret code for basic drives, for wishes to be fulfilled. 'Going back' in Freud's way, seemed to reduce people's dreams to a set of rather unattractive, self-centred needs. He wondered why

Above: In dreams of a sexual nature it is interesting to see if natural or artificial images are used to express the dreamer's attitude.

dreams so often seemed to inspire people, to encourage them in their waking lives to do bigger and better things.

He was fascinated by the strange array of mysterious objects and creatures that occur in dreams. Freud's theory seemed to relate all parts of a dream to something inside the dreamer's own make-up. But to Jung this did not account for the pictures which appeared to come from a fantasy world outside the dreamer's everyday view of life.

Jung and the Collective Unconscious

Jung's solution to this mystery was that all human beings have two parts to their unconscious. Freud had looked at the part which hides personal, instinctive urges away. Jung now identified a part that, is filled with strange primitive imaginings, which are common to everyone everywhere.

For example, why do all children love stories of witches, ogres and fairies when they have no real-life experience of these creatures at all? Why do people invent monsters in their dreams when there are no such things in the world? Jung suggested that we all share a Collective Unconscious, for we all respond to these basic fancies.

Many civilizations in all parts of the world have created exactly the same pictures in dreams, fairy stories and myths and they are readily understood by people from another country or from another age.

> 'I was sitting on top of Popocatepetl, playing a card game with three friends. Out of the volcano came beautiful soap bubbles which rose into the air, then floated down the conical sides of the volcano to join the sea of bubbles stretching away on every side as far as the eye could see. The sun came up and the bubbles glistened iridescently, first mauvy-blue, then peachy, then watery green, then all sorts of mother-of-pearl colours shimmering together.'
> Student, female, 20

Throughout time, various nations have created remarkably similar stories about their heroes. Moses was found in the bulrushes; Jesus was born in an equally humble stable. The Greek goddess Aphrodite was born out of the sea just as the first ancient Inca ruler came out of a lake. There is no apparent reason for this similarity in legend, folklore and religion. Jung suggests that everyone has a natural tendency to think in these globally familiar ways.

Jung first drew attention to people's fascination with monsters. These fearful images seem to come from a universally shared mythology, equally recognizable to people from all civilizations.

CHRIS YATES

Archetypes

These universal ideas were termed Archetypes, which means the original of a type. They are basic ancient beliefs which, according to Jung, we inherit rather than learn. So old and general are they that we do not need to ask what they mean when they appear in the mind's eye; we simply recognize them deep down without having to question them. These Archetypes are the language—the 'secret code'—of dreams.

Putting the theory into practice, look at the familiar figure of the hero. There are many instances in classical myths, such as the adventures of Hercules, Odysseus or Prometheus; in Britain there was the ideal of King Arthur and Sir Lancelot or St. George slaying the Dragon; in Australia Ned Kelly became a hero of mythic proportions, and there are countless examples from the Old West of the United States. Even in modern dress, the hero persists in comic strip characters such as Superman. Jung is simply saying that no one has to tell you what a hero is. You know what the person stands for as soon as you see the type.

Most of the Archetypes to which Jung drew attention were of a religious nature. Jung was for a long time Freud's disciple, and when he broke away from him because he disagreed with his views, he also developed a great interest in eastern religions. In turn people have disagreed violently with Jung, saying that this Collective Unconscious is a lot of mumbo-jumbo and cannot be proved scientifically. At least Freud had some factual basis for his beliefs. But in one sense the Jungian view is easy to accept, because he also believed that the Archetypes, as they appear in dreams, are reflections of ourselves. Many religions have a similar philosophy when they say God is really inside the individual.

But what if a dream contains a friend that you can recognize or even no people at all? Jung maintained that the friend is there because he or she reflects part of yourself. A room may stand for your own mind—the inside of yourself. In this way, all the Jungian Archetypes are simply representations of the human condition. Where they come from no one can say, but they are made concrete in the world of dreams, appearing like well-known actors on a private stage. Monsters are a 'projection', a representation of our own innermost fears. Heroes are a real-life realization of our own tendency to do good, brave deeds. A witchwoman—another familiar Archetype—represents the destructive feminine impulse in human beings. Because these Archetypes are showing us to ourselves, they are easily recognizable, even by children. No one needs to explain to a child that the giant in Jack and the Beanstalk is all bad or that the Fairy Godmother in Cinderella is completely trustworthy. In the actual stories neither of these characteristics is proved: it is just known and accepted by the children hearing the tale. The same is true of the Archetypes of dreams. We do not read them up in books for they come naturally to mind. There is a mystery about the source of the Archetypes: if you are religious you will find it easy to believe that they spring from a force beyond human understanding. Others might accept that there is a basic energy in human nature which has over the

> 'My girlfriend and I are in a cottage in the country — not our real one, which stands by itself — but in one that is part of a group, but fairly isolated. There is a huge bomb explosion; the cottage of some people we know has been blown up and is burning ferociously. We know that they are dead, so we go indoors. But then we realize that the flames are spreading into our neighbors' houses, closer and closer to ours. I throw water on — and then buckets of pins and needles — to douse the flames. It is very powerful and scary.'
> Financial journalist, male, 32

centuries responded to certain unconscious forces. These are revealed in the Archetypes.

Archetypal symbols

One thing is sure—Archetypes occur time and time again in the same form. These are termed symbols. Just as a child instantly 'knows' the giant or the fairy godmother, so we all 'know' the meaning of the symbols. Take the story of the Garden of Eden. Eve is persuaded to eat an apple by an evil serpent. Everyone knows what the apple stands for, without having it spelled out for them. 'Forbidden fruit' is a symbol we can all understand. Another example is the standing stone. It is used to suggest permanence in many forms: in Stonehenge, in gravestones or in monuments like the Cenotaph in London or the Washington Monument. In the Bible, Jesus calls his disciple Peter the 'Stone' or 'Rock', for that is the translation of his name from the Greek. Everyone recognizes the meaning behind the idea—even in today's conversation we refer to a reliable man with the phrase, 'He's as solid as a rock'.

Unknown Archetypes

More surprisingly, Jung discovered that people can dream using certain symbols without being at all clear of the Archetypal meaning at the time. People seem to inherit certain motifs in their thinking patterns without being aware of it. In one case, a girl dreamed of crossing a bleak moor with a good friend. On the way they met a large number of ape-like creatures with funny, friendly faces. They all proceeded together—arm in arm, cuddling up to the apes—towards their destination: a beautiful fairy-tale city glistening in the sunlight.

Only on thinking over the dream, which seemed to have no connection with any events in real life (no visits to the zoo!), did the girl discover that the ape-monkey is a very common symbol in eastern religions for the Self—the intuitive, emotional part of a person as opposed to the intellectual, logical part. A picture in a book of the Hindu monkey god Hanuman was so uncannily like the ape-monkey of her dream that the girl was very surprised. The friend was probably included in the dream because the dreamer admired her for her creative abilities and her warm personality. In Jungian terms, it all added up to a message that she should let the intuitive part of her nature guide her towards her goal—symbolized by the city—not just her thinking, logical self. Jung has written about many such incidents that occurred when he was treating his patients. If you cannot think of any private recollection connected with a symbol, it can be very helpful in your own attempts to understand dreams to try to find out something about the universal cultural symbolism described in the case above.

Anima or Animus: your dream reflection

Jung continued to explore the idea that dreams reflect the Self: one of the most fascinating ideas he put forward was that we have an opposite side to our personalities. In men, this appears as an idealized female figure called the Anima, in women, as a male, the Animus. In contrast, Freud would have believed that the appearance of a male

figure in a woman's dream represented sexual desires for someone, but Jung suggested that it could be the male aspect of her own character. We associate this with aggressive, extrovert, decisive qualities—some bad, some good. In a way, dreaming about male movie stars may even show a woman some aspect of her own male character. In men, the Anima is embodied in all the poets' ideas of an inspiring muse, who gives them the power to write beautiful things. In religion, she is the perfect figure of Mary, the mother of Jesus; in Chinese myth, she is the fertility goddess, Kuan-Yin; in classical times she was Aestarti, Venus or Ceres; nowadays she could be Marilyn Monroe, Maria Callas or even Queen Elizabeth II.

> 'I have a vast number of sales reports to make—but I haven't got round to it and I've forgotten what they're even supposed to be about. There's a great compulsion to get them done—but then suddenly I'm off on another business trip, involving a great deal of packing and preparation, none of which has been done and I have a ship to catch in a matter of hours. I always end up wondering whether I can conceivably get a car to get to the port on time.'
> Retired salesman, 60

The Persona and the Shadow

Two other parts of your self can appear in dreams in a symbolic form.
The first is the Persona, which Jung explains as the character or image you project outwardly. This acting figure who faces the world and says what it should do is often not your real self. In dreams, your Persona rather than your real self often takes part. You must recognize that this is not your innermost honest being. Jung tells the story of a woman who in real life was impossibly stubborn and full of fixed opinions. No one could ever win against her in an argument or even get her to admit she was wrong. One night she dreamed that she was going to a very important social occasion. On the doorstep, her hostess greeted her and said delightedly that all her friends were ready waiting inside. Then she led her through a doorway—into a cowshed! The dreamer's unconscious was giving her a picture of what her Persona

or image was really like and which she would not consciously admit to herself. Finally, a very helpful aid to understanding dreams from the Jungian point of view is contained in the Archetype of the Shadow. This is just what it suggests. It is the other side of your personality which does not see the light of day very often. It does not necessarily mean the evil or bad part of you, it might just be the secret part you feel least able to bring out into real life. It might be tender, imaginative and romantic and so you keep it lurking behind an agressive facade. It might also be truly destructive, as characterized vividly by Robert Louis Stevenson in *Dr. Jekyll and Mr. Hyde*—a story which came to the author during a dream.

The Shadow can be good or bad and can make your dreams very confused because you have to decide if the dream is about your outward personality or the Shadow behind. But life is pretty complicated too, and dreams reflect the conflicts experienced in it. It is interesting that small children seem to have an instinctive knowledge about the fundamental Archetypes of the Persona and the Shadow, for at some stage most play with an imaginary friend—who somehow seems to be the one who causes all the trouble in the household!

Although at first sight the theories of Freud and Jung seem to be poles apart and quite irreconcilable, they are not basically very contradictory. What matters most is that if a dream points out a problem area, exactly which way you take it will depend on your personal circumstances. Other symbols in the dream, especially those of a personal remembrance or of an Archetypal, general meaning, will help to make the central issue clear. Some people are more prone to follow Freud than Jung or the other way round. People who regularly visit a Freudian psychoanalyst tend to dream with lots of sexual pictures, while people who become interested in Jung start to fill their nights with magical visions of weird beasts and religious figures. The mind is very suggestive and responds to outside influences in surprisingly quick ways.

Dreams as problem solvers

Most modern dream researchers have established themselves on the basic principles of either Freud or Jung, and most have tried to find a less extreme position. J. A. Hadfield is a British psychologist who believes that dreams are basically problem-solving. He pays

particular attention to the fact that over a period of time, dreams will concentrate on a specific problem area trying out one possible solution after another until one dream comes to a realization of the issue. A simple example is the habit of dreaming about an accident. Drivers tend to have the same dream over and over again. At first the dream will make the accident take place as if realizing the dreamer's worst fears. Then gradually the content changes and the dreamer finally sees himself actually avoiding the accident by fast reaction and good steering. The dreams have worked off the driver's sense of anxiety and possible guilt about his behaviour on the road. So your dream may warn you where you are going wrong and why. It may reveal parts of yourself, consciously overlooked, which you should take into account in the future.

> 'I am on a paddle steamer—it's hot and sunny. Snow White and the Seven Dwarfs are sitting in deck chairs, surrounded by wicker travelling trunks. I go inside into a dim bathroom with no windows. The walls are covered with green tiles and the bulb is broken, leaving a glowing filament. Everything is dusty and dirty, and when I turn the taps on, rusty nuts and bolts come out.' Girl, 8.

Act out your dreams

An American psychoanalyst, Fritz Perls, developed the problem-solving aspect of dreams in an unusual way. One of his teaching methods was to have people act out the events of their dreams as if they really happened. It can be surprisingly revealing, and sometimes very amusing to do this.

Perls once had a teenage girl patient who had dreamed several times about her mother but had no idea what the drift of her thoughts intended. She thought she had a good relationship with her mother, all things considered. Perls asked her to talk as if she were the mother-figure in the dream and then to reply as the daughter. It rapidly emerged in this invented conversation that the voice she gave the mother was louder, more decisive and altogether more on top of the situation. As 'herself', the girl seemed unable to reply and changed physically as she acted, hanging her head and mumbling her words. Clearly, the girl did not really feel that she had found her feet. Nor was she free of her mother's domination, although she had said aloud that she got along with her mother pretty well. She automatically assumed the hangdog, feeble Persona of her dream.

You can try this simple experiment yourself—even if the dream is about objects, not people. For instance if the dream has a tree in it, why not imagine what kind of tree *you* are: 'I'm a tall thin sapling. I may not look very strong, but actually I can withstand winds and rain well, because I can bend and not break'. Over a period of time, you can build up a very revealing commentary, especially if you keep a journal of these thoughts.

The off-line brain

If however you dislike the idea of so much imagination being involved in understanding your dreams, you may prefer to consider the very interesting theory put forward by another British specialist, Dr. Christopher Evans. Remember that the unconscious has been described as a 'sorting house', taking in all kinds of information, sifting and absorbing it and then telling you in a dream how things stand in your real self. Dr. Evans has developed the idea of the sorting-house into a comparison with a computer. A computer is just a very elaborate calculating machine whose operation is controlled by large numbers of 'programs'. Programs are nothing more than special instructions which tell the computer what to do. With modern computers these programs have to be continually revised and brought up-to-date, a process which is best done when the system is (to use a technical term) 'off-line'. When a computer is off-line it is not switched off but rather uncoupled from its environment. Plenty of activity can go on inside but it doesn't interact with the external world. You might say that it's a little like a library which is put out of bounds to the public at regular periods so that the staff can do some cataloguing and rearranging. If computers don't have their programs revised in these off-line periods then they get muddled, out-of-date, inefficient and ultimately breakdown. Dr. Evans argues that the brain itself is a computer—a biological rather than an electromechanical one—and it too must be controlled by programs. Furthermore these programs must also be revised and updated and this must be done when the system is 'off-line'. So when we are asleep our brain is off-line and dreams represent the brain sifting through its

SANDERS

old programs, rewriting them, discarding dud ones and putting in new ones. We do this, Dr. Evans believes, for a large part of the sleeping period and it is this program revision that is the basis of true dreaming. The kind of 'dreams' we remember over breakfast in the morning are the fragments of the major programs which were being rewritten during the night and which were interrupted for one reason or another as the conscious mind briefly came awake.

If you look at each individual incident or object in a dream, it will relate to some new information, some newly-absorbed experience in your recent past. It might be from words read in a newspaper, from pictures seen on

Women in dreams may not only be the subject of sexual fantasy, but alternatively a symbol of the feminine aspects of a man's nature.

television, overheard remarks or friendly conversations. All these bits and pieces will be sifted and processed by the computer-brain in sleep.

All these theories, old and new, are evidence of the vast amount of research that is going on at present to understand the significance of dreams. No matter which view appeals to you most, at least consider that dreams are not completely random and absurd. They are proof that the brain is a complex, delicate organ with a potential that has barely been recognized.

The language of dreams

Dreams give their message in a direct, non-verbal way: they present a series of ideas inside your sleeping brain. Some of the ideas come in a very clear visual sequence which you can recall in the morning and relate to someone else almost as if the whole experience had really happened or had been read as part of a book. At other times the pictures are so fragmentary and jumbled that you can only remember one particular action.

Psychologists attach a great deal of importance to the way things are presented in dreams. To understand the message, it is vital to know what to look for. For instance, if someone you are talking to yawns while saying 'how interesting' and looks over your left shoulder, he is trying to tell you that the whole subject is really a bore. Dreams often use the same mannerisms we use in conversation and these tricks of speech give a clue to what is really being conveyed.

The meaning of symbols

First, learn to distinguish between symbols and images in your dreams. They are both dream pictures, but the possible meanings are very different. Symbols say something to everyone. They have a general significance which can be grasped by all people everywhere. **The 'magic man'** is a traditional symbol, of which many examples can be found. Merlin the Magician, the Wizard of Oz, the witch-doctors of Africa or the medicine men of American Indian tribes have the same powers.

The Garden of Paradise is another well-known symbol. This is a vision of a perfect place where everything is good and nothing goes wrong. People of all eras have found ways to express this symbolically. There is the Garden of Eden in the Bible, the Elysian Fields of Greek myth, and Mahomet's beautiful Paradise of the Islamic faith, where lovely girls or 'houris' wait with musk perfume, wine and the promise of love for the faithful. Nowadays, the same ideal is used by travel brochures to lure holidaymakers to that perfect resort where the sun always shines, the sea is clear and blue, the beach isn't crowded

and there's a never-ending supply of exotic food, drink and beautiful people. **A ship sailing over an empty ocean** symbolizes man's progress through life. It is a good example of combining more than one symbol to form a widely-understood situation. The ship represents his society—his way of organizing with other people, some system against possible chaos in the world. The sea stands for the age-old unknown forces of the universe or the creative mass which lies unformed below the surface of the mind. This way of imagining life

> 'I set out on a journey with a large open egg tray balanced on the palm of my hand and a carafe of wine clutched in the other. The terrain was rocky and the narrow footpath lined with bushes. The pace was brisk and I had to concentrate very hard not to break the eggs as I tripped up and down the uneven path. When I got to my destination the eggs just broke of their own accord. I thought: "Well I still have the wine". Then I noticed I no longer had it. Concentrating so hard on the eggs, I had left the wine somewhere along the way. So I turned back to find it.'
> **Fashion journalist, 36, female**

comes to us in the stories of Odysseus travelling the seas in search of home or in Jason's hunt for the Golden Fleece. In the Middle Ages, the 'Ship of Fools' was a favourite theme, characterizing all the types of people you could meet on your journey through life. Perhaps the familiarity of this symbol accounts for its favour with politicians, who are constantly talking about the 'ship of state' and the need for a 'firm hand at the helm'.

If you find something in your dreams that is not clear to you from your own experience of life or from immediate past events you can recall, then try to think more broadly of its possible symbolic meaning. The paradise sym-

bol just mentioned is quite common. Any dream of a beautiful calm place, not necessarily a Garden of Eden in the religious sense, may have overtones of this general symbolic meaning. Sailing on a ship may have nothing to do with sea voyage you have actually experienced: it may simply be a way of representing your progress through life. The phrase 'all at sea' will perhaps help you to understand the function of this symbol.

Images in dreams

An image works rather differently from a symbol. This is simply a more accurate way of referring to a picture. Dreams work in images: they take an idea, a thought or feeling and turn it into an exact picture or image to present to you in sleep. They are generally more commonplace than symbols—like offices, shops and all the paraphenalia of day-to-day life. This word is properly used in the phrase, 'He's the spitting image of his father'—that is, he looks exactly like him.

Suppose someone is 'up in the clouds' in your opinion. In your dream, you may well have an image of him actually sitting on a cloud. Studying hard for exams might show up in a dream as someone being force-fed or sitting in front of a huge plate of food. When you 'can't take any more in', your dream says so with an image of the feeling. If you feel you cannot see the wood for the trees in your life, perhaps you will dream of being lost in a giant forest.

Not all dreams are just images of well-known phrases like this: sometimes your dream invents a new image or picture as a way of saying something. Men who have trouble relating to women often dream of she-monsters. This is a vivid image of their feelings, showing how they respond emotionally to the female. Their shyness may really be a fear that women are too clever or too passionate and will take them over completely.

Images can be very amusing because they are so apt and direct in their message. A young girl who was beginning to visit a psychoanalyst to work out a particular difficulty in her life

Above: Background in dreams is very important. Exotic, faraway places suggest freedom and a lack of inhibition. A desirable and inviting girl is of course a standard male fantasy!

dreamed that she arrived at her analyst's house and found lots of underwear all over the waiting room. It was being aired on the radiators and on chairs round the heater. This could be interpreted as an image of the girl's own misgivings about 'washing her dirty linen' in public, expressing a wish that her analyst would spill a few secrets in return just to even the balance! Of course, this is just one possible interpretation: remember that the image of

ladies' underwear has strong sexual overtones as well.

The tricks of dream language

Once you can begin to look at the apparent 'story' of your dream as a series of images, then you will find it much easier to study. Try to evaluate each picture in its own right, as well as the overall effect of the dream. When you recognize images and see the possible symbolic value of some of them, then you can try to supply the following advice about the tricks or mannerisms of dream language. These points to watch were first recognized by Sigmund Freud, whose book, *The Interpretation*

of Dreams is still considered to be one of the finest and most valuable studies in the field.

Condensation

More than likely, you have already discovered that any one image in a dream can mean a number of things. Do not worry or be put off if several different ideas spring to mind at once it only shows how rich in suggestion and how powerful in meaning the dream language can be. Freud had one fascinating example of this characteristic, which he called condensation. A woman dreamed about some beetles trapped in a small box. At first she thought the

image had been suggested by something she had seen the day before—a moth had fallen into a glass of water. This might indeed have provoked the choice of image but does not go deep enough into why, of all the petty details from the day, that should have come up in her dream. The woman was then reminded of her daughter's hobby of collecting butterflies and this drew her back to memories of her own youth. Finally, Freud helped her to work through to the hidden or latent meaning of her dream. She was concerned about her husband's waning interest in sex and she knew that a well-known aphrodisiac called *cantharides* is made from crushed beetles.

Another image in the dream helped the woman to put two and two together, for she had also dreamed about open and shut windows. This immediately reminded her of a running battle she had with her husband about fresh air in the bedroom, rather than all the windows being shut. That led to a consideration of her relationship with her husband, and the underlying meaning of the beetle image came clear.

What if you do not know all the possible meanings of an image? After all, not everyone knows about aphrodisiacs made from beetle juice! The woman worked round to her own meaning simply by seeing connections—or condensations—in the beetle image of her dream. Thinking about her daughter's hobby reminded her of her own youth and attractiveness and called back memories of old romances. This in itself would have led to the heart of the problem, even if she had stopped there with the beetle image. Remember also that dreams are more often than not about things that worry us. It is not usually necessary to dig very deeply before the problem springs to mind. It is only in serious cases of mental anxiety or disturbance, when the cause is buried in the unconscious, that a lot of pain and effort is required to find it— and that calls for professional help.

Displacement

Almost as important as the condensing process is displacement, when the real concern of the dream is pushed into a small image. The images are skirting round the issue in order to avoid presenting a direct, head-on picture of the problem. If the dream becomes too clear it often turns into a nightmare

Left: The mood generated in a dream is very significant. The landscape could be gentle but is there an air of menace?

which wakes the dreamer up. Freud also thought that dreams are thus disguised to avoid upsetting the 'Conscience' part of the mind—the part that guards the basic thoughts and tries to stop them coming out—but nowadays, like most of Freud's ideas, this view is disputed.

Suppose you are worried about a relative, such as your sister. You might dream of a woman being involved in a car crash. This stranger may look totally different from your real-life sister, except that she is wearing the same glasses or a dress in a style your real sister prefers. This should be enough to tell you the true subject of your dream.

Freud was right in saying that this displacing device occurs when a part of you thinks you are doing something wrong. Suppose you are attracted to someone but you think should not be. You may have a very sexy dream involving a complete stranger, but his name may be similar, his clothing—or even a word he says—may recall the true object of your feelings. But if this were always true, then you would never have very explicit, clear dreams whose questionable parts are not disguised, and you would wake up far less often than you do from disturbing dreams.

A stranger or a shadow in a dream, incidentally, may have some symbolic meaning as discussed in the previous chapter. These figures can stand for sides of your own nature or personality that you do not know or refuse to acknowledge. Obviously, the other images in a dream will help you to decide which is the correct way of assessing them.

Reversal

An amusing trick to try, if a dream obstinately refuses to yield any meaning to you whatsoever, is to turn it round completely. Reversal is a common feature of the dream language. If you dream you are walking over a carpet in muddy boots, then why not consider: 'Am I the carpet, being walked over by other people?' The dream image may be saying, 'Don't be a doormat', in an upside-down way. The feeling of the dream may help. You would probably feel upset or indignant during a dream of this sort, which would certainly reflect the true meaning.

Killing or harming a child in a dream is a common worry for parents. But this too might be reversal; they hope very much that no harm of any sort will come to the family. But according to Freud, it might also be a wish-fulfilling

dream, recalling some moment of intense exasperation when a parent does feel like 'killing' a child. It is better to let off steam in this way in a dream than to harbour the feeling so that it affects your real experience of life.

Killing your own father or mother however does not follow the reversal principle. This merely shows in strong terms your attempts to break away from parental authority. You want to stand on your own feet and be independent. A parent can be concealed in an image of another kind of authority—a king, a ruler of a state or your boss at work.

A more Jungian approach might also consider whether you wish to rebel against some dominant part of yourself, reflected in an authoritative person.

Compensation

Jung also elaborated on the idea of reversal, believing that one of the main functions of a dream is to provide compensation for your real self. If you are a harrassed housewife, you may dream of being a glamorous, cool career woman. A ruthless businessman will tend to put himself in the place of a butterfly collector or a romantic intellectual in an ivory tower. A shy girl will dream of holding court in a circle of admiring boys. All these dreams are making up for the failings or unfulfilled needs of an everyday self.

Animism

Bear in mind also that if a person in your dream seems particularly wonderful, magical or idealized, it may come under one of those symbolic meanings already discussed.

A very beautiful, tender woman in a man's dream might represent his own finer, female instincts—what Jungian's call the Anima. Similarly, a sympathetic, courageous male figure might stand for a woman's own braver nature —her Animus.

Dreams have a habit of showing abstract things or feelings in the more visual form of people or animals. Bravery, just mentioned, will become a brave man; tenderness, a loving woman; Freud called this trick 'animism'. The same term is often used to describe the way objects are given human or animal properties by primitive peoples, for in their waking, day-to-day life they too turn abstract things into people or animals. The wind becomes 'the big man who blows'. Try to think broadly about this kind of image in dreams, for they work in the same way.

A policeman is often the most familiar character to appear in our dreams as the voice of conscience.

A devil figure may represent feelings or urges which you think are wrong but somehow cannot control.

An angel will act as the voice of good, as if from the nobler side of your nature or from your heartfelt faith in something.

A tramp will be an image for some unacceptable part of you or for something of which you are ashamed.

A gipsy will stand for some wild, impulsive, out-of-the-ordinary desire that you have lurking about inside you.

A baby will not just stand for birth or for your own desire to have children. It can just as well signify abstract things such as ideas or creative imaginings. A good example of this was a young man's dream about giving birth to perfectly-formed but very small babies. It was not some peculiar urge to be a woman! His profession was graphic designing and the babies stood for his wish to produce 'perfectly conceived' finished artwork or design ideas.

The cat image normally stands for supposedly feminine qualities such as intuition.

Dogs not unnaturally act as images for more traditionally masculine attributes such as adventurousness, aggression or faithfulness. This is an image that can contain many different abstract references, so you have to consider your own particular view of dogs (especially pets you know well) and add those ideas to the suggestions given here. For example, a scruffy, mongrel-type dog could indicate a low opinion of someone—possibly yourself—coming out in your dreams.

Other animals that commonly occur as dream images are wolves (fear, sexual aggression, hunger), rats (despicable, underhand people or feelings), rabbits (fertility or soft, easily-hurt characters) lambs (sacrifice, innocence, purity) and sheep (easily swayed, timid people). Sometimes the very nature of an animalistic image will help you to see the true meaning.

Horses for example are frequently chosen by female dreamers to symbolize the act of sex. A wild, strong stallion with a flowing mane is a beautiful way of imagining the power and force of sexual feeling. Notice how different this is from that other favourite sexual symbol—the automobile.

The car is sleek, powerful and shiny, but it is also automatic and mechanical underneath. If you dream of being driven by someone or sitting in the passenger seat, this indicates a more passive role in the situation. You should look into the dream to see if taking a more positive, outgoing attitude is being suggested to you.

Jokes and puns

Not all dreams take a serious approach to your experiences. For some reason, people find it difficult to accept jokes or puns in dreams at first, as if they believe that dreams must always be intense, mysterious and earnest underneath. But some unusual experiments have proved that we use word-play even in sleep.

> 'I was wearing a backless bathing suit and I had to have a school photograph taken in those strange rows they make you sit in. For some reason I had a bra on underneath — and as the costume was backless you could see the bra at the back. So I wanted to find a place to take it off, just a public lavatory or something. But either I couldn't find one or if I got to one, there was always someone waiting outside and I was feeling a bit coy about the whole thing, so I was having a terrible time. I think I eventually did get the bra off and I felt much happier, then I went and sat down in my place with an enormous sweater over the bathing suit so that the whole thing was pointless anyway, with sort of little pink knees showing and wondering whether anyone would mind about the fact that I didn't have a school dress on.'
> Package designer, female, 24

Ian Oswald, the British dream researcher, describes how the whispering of certain names to sleeping people, for instance the name of an ex-girlfriend or a former work colleague, will draw a response from the dreamer. A girl who heard the word Robert inserted a rabbit into her dream! The brain seems to mishear the word and includes an image whose word sound is close to the word actually said. Don't dismiss word-play or punning when looking for the meaning of a dream image. Someone who places the events of a dream in a football field for instance may in fact mean 'field' in its metaphorical sense, as in the 'field' of medicine or academics.

Psychologists find that people sometimes see a joke that is not apparent to anyone else. The dreamer recognizes that a figure represents someone known personally, because of a silly word or a ludicrous situation. If a dream contained the image of a king seated on a throne in the act of re-folding the Sunday newspaper and grumbling about it, then a family member might know instantly that the royal figure was Dad, who always complained about everyone else getting the paper first and losing his sports page!

Absurd dreams

An extension of dreams with jokes or puns are those which are at the time absurd. You wake up thinking, 'What a silly situation!' Sometimes the absurdity is simply the result of a lack of time-span or proper connections. This is a characteristic of dreams in general. They are like films that are badly made, jumping suddenly from one scene to the next, from one image to another without proper observance of the conventional logic of real life. This explains why dreams often contain absurd mixtures of people. Suppose your grandfather is mixed up in a dream with some of your close friends and neighbours, when in reality he died ten years ago. Freud suggests that this is as if you were saying to yourself, 'What would my grandfather say about this if he were alive?' Your dream, with no respect for time or individuals, simply makes that suggestion real. Even if you can't imagine why you should think such a thing—even unconsciously— stop and wonder if there are any characteristics about your grandfather (or whoever it is) that have some relation to the subject matter of your dream. It can be quite revealing.

Although it is sometimes upsetting or distressing to dream about a relative or dear friend who is dead, this explanation will help to put it into perspective. You may be bringing that person back because they held views or values that

Nudity is an expression of a desire to be frank and open without hiding behind a social facade. It can turn up in the oddest situations—but are they really so absurd? A tiger for instance is a clear image of the power of sexuality; a policeman and obviously a priest stand for the force of conscience. In this context, death, in the form of a funeral cortège, could stand for the dreamer's suppression of real feelings.

are significant in your present life. However, Freud also points out that ridicule can be a form of criticism. If you place someone near to you in an absurd position then you may be letting out some critical opinion you formerly kept to yourself, possibly for the best of reasons, like love or a sense of respect. Do not confuse absurd dreams with others which are simply odd or peculiar. Absurd dreams have a strong feeling of mockery attached to them *at the time.* You often feel that things are absurd during the dream itself. Most dreams only seem silly when you wake up and think about them in the cold light of day.

Nakedness. A common dream of this type that causes embarrassed laughs is that of nakedness. 'I walked right down the main street in broad daylight with nothing on, but I didn't seem to care.'

The interesting point to notice is the lack of any sense of absurdity or shame at the time. Freud believed these dreams were purely wish-fulfilling, satisfying a basic exhibitionist streak in everyone. However, Jung and many other psychologists have come to accept this kind of image as an expression of a desire to be frank, open and true to ourselves. If there is any feeling of fear attached to it, then clearly the message is that you are afraid of what people might think if you express your real views, behave naturally or lower your defences.

It is interesting to see how social convention makes us think that being stripped or caught without clothes is a sign of humiliation, shame or degradation. This dream image is really using the idea in a much more basic, true way. How about the traditional story of

'Lion devouring a horse' by the celebrated 18th century British painter, George Stubbs, is a powerful impression of the destructive capacity of aggressive or sexual drives. Both animals are world-wide symbols of these instincts.

the Emperor's new clothes—is it a joke against the court who fell for appearances, or against the Emperor for being so silly that he walked about in the nude?

Swimming is frequently connected with nakedness dreams. By now you will probably be thinking ahead to its possible meanings. People talk about being 'in the swim', or in old-fashioned schoolgirl slang, things went 'swimmingly'. Add to this the ideas already explained about the sea or ocean symbol and it is easy to see that swimming represents being at ease with life or being at one with your feelings and desires, pushing ahead with energy and excitement. Adler would say that swimming with effort stands for the urge for power or achievement; thus swimming upstream or against the tide can be taken exactly as the words suggest. You are going against popular opinion or trying to cope with troublesome issues. If the dream includes reaching land after the struggle, it may be a way of encouraging you in your aims.

Naked swimming can also suggest sexual fulfilment, as you will no doubt know if you have ever watched those old films with native girls splashing around, wide-eyed and flower-decked, while gun-laden soldiers or pith-helmeted hunters peer through the bushes! (Freud also said a great deal about the sexual imagery of guns and other weapons.)

Repetition

At the opposite end of the scale from absurdity or apparent nonsense is the intense feeling that is generated by repetition. This way of making a point in a dream is the most easy to identify. It is explained simply as a way of saying 'very much so' in images.

Climbing up a hill which seems endlessly steep and arduous is a way of saying 'Getting along in this life is very, very hard going'. It could be that the dream is an expression of fear or doubt about a particular goal you have in sight. You might pause and consider if pursuing the aim is really as important as all the effort it will cost.

A very long journey by train or bus embodies the same idea. 'Life is tedious', the dream is saying. It is implicit in the train image that catching or missing it relates to your views about life. Are you missing out on good opportunities; do you worry about success? An endlessly repeated attempt to catch a train would suggest a state of anxiety or tension about getting on in the world. Perhaps the dream is warning you to relax a little and not take things so seriously. Remember that mechanical means of transport also suggest an automatic, driving power in your life. We say someone has 'gone off the rails' if things go wrong for him. An endless train journey, especially if you are a passive individual sitting quietly in a carriage watching everything flit by, suggests a humdrum existence in which you let yourself be carried along. But your dream is telling you that somewhere deep down you know this is not really what you want.

Lucid dreams

Sometimes you will have a dream in which you are passive in a different way. You stand back from the events taking place, saying to yourself, 'I *know* this is a dream, but I'll let it go on'. Other people decide exactly the same thing but enter the dream, changing what happens in it. It is as if they say, 'I don't like this part of the dream; let's change it to something else'. These are called lucid dreams and offer two possible explanations. If you realize it is a dream but stand back and do nothing, then this is a way of keeping the situation at arm's length. You do not enter into the experience of the

> 'I remember sitting in a cafe with a friend. The cafe is a very strange place with lots of different levels and stairs. The table we are at is beside a window which looks out over a large walled garden. The garden seems quite a long way down and is ablaze with flowers and plants of every description. Suddenly I am no longer in the cafe but in the garden, there are lots of loaves of bread about. Then I see a large, green crocodile. I start to climb the wall, which is easy (but I seem to be getting nowhere fast). I eventually reach the top and find myself in a wasteland. I wander off and walk miles until I come to a river. There is a bridge over the river and I see a policeman and another man.'
> **Illustrator, 25, female**

problem even in sleep. This might be a way of showing that in reality you behave in just the same way—by not facing up to issues or meeting them head-on.

If on the other hand you seem to direct the course of the dream, changing the 'plot' and making things happen, then it is possible that the dream is being helpful or therapeutic. You are exploring various endings or trying out different ways of resolving your real-life difficulties. Dreaming of making things come to life exemplifies the kind of image found in a lucid dream. It is a beautiful way of suggesting that there are latent, unused powers inside you that are beginning to blossom and come out. You should be encouraged by such

a promising dream and act on it as positively as you can!

Secondary revision

The final point to consider when you are looking at dream images is a little more complicated but worth the effort if you find that most dreams respond to your analysis, but just a few evade you. It often happens that a dream seems so clear and recognizable that the meaning is straightforward and comes out at once. This is especially likely if the dream has similarities with a wish or favourite ambition. Knowledge of these ideal hopes and fantasies keeps a public relations man's salary healthy, when he plays up to them in his advertisements! Suppose you dream of moving into a beautiful house, furnished in exquisite taste with everything you have ever wanted. Whatever else happens in this dream, you will be likely to wake up and say, 'Oh well, that's clear, it was just one of my wish-fulfilling dreams', and then forget all about it. Of course you want a house like that—many people do. But dreams are rarely quite so simple. You will probably overlook other parts of the dream in order to fit the whole experience into your favourite fantasy. Freud described this process as 'secondary revision' and maintained that it leads people into making quick, superficial judgements about the contents of their dreams. Look more closely at that house again. Were there any details, such as going down into the basement or climbing upstairs to look at the view? Were there any objects you noticed as you passed—any clothes in cupboards or rubbish left neatly in a corner? It may not always work, because dreams fade so quickly, especially if you made a quick snap judgement and put the thought aside. But if you can go back over the dream and look at the finer details, you will probably surprise yourself as new interpretations spring to mind.

Looking into your dreams

Do not worry if you feel you will not remember all these different points when you try looking at your own dreams. Even if you only remember one or two the first time, the rest will follow. It is much better to take a relaxed view and simply mull over a few thoughts. You will certainly fail if you sit down with a long list and a red pencil, taking an academic approach to the task. Dreams are natural things and they should not be forced into an intellectual guessing game.

What is sleep and how do we dream?

When you go to sleep you do not merely lose awareness of the world around you. Pronounced physiological changes also take place. The body's temperature is lowered, the heart's pulse rate is slower, and various bodily functions such as digestion are measurably reduced.

It seems that there could be certain areas of the brain which need constant stimulation to keep us awake that is, conscious. Sleep is the state which occurs when these areas cease to be stimulated.

No one can survive without regular periods of sleep, even though it may seem a waste of time—especially to children—to spend about a third of a lifetime in what appears to be a state of 'nothingness'. Furthermore, sleep is required *at regular intervals*: it is not as useful to the body to have 4 hours of sleep one night and 30 hours the next. The body has learned to work by a 24-hour clock and finds it difficult to forget. This clock, based on the movement of the earth round the sun and the consequent periods of light and dark, is known as the 'circadian rhythm'.

There is some truth in the general belief that working on night shift produces less satisfactory work than the normal daytime periods. The body takes many days, even weeks, to get out of the circadian rhythm, and during that time physical co-ordination, alertness and other manifestations of mental ability function less effectively. Anyone who has travelled between continents by jet will know how difficult it is to adjust to a new time scale. Even the relatively simple 'hop' between New York and London means a 5-hour difference in time and many people feel disoriented for several days, even if they appear to have caught up with lost sleep.

In general, the brain needs regular doses of sleep to continue making judgements or decisions and carry on other thinking processes. Experiments have shown that sleeplessness does not impair physical activity—but it does hinder concentration. People become increasingly vague the longer they go without sleep, eventually suffering from hallucinations—literally dreaming with their eyes open.

The activity of sleep

When asleep, the body and brain are not completely dead to the world or unconscious. The body is kept going by the activity of the autonomic nervous system, which controls the essential 'life support systems' of the heart, digestion, cell repair and replacement and so on, which continue during sleep. The senses also continue to be active to a certain degree: when an alarm clock rings, a part of your head registers the sounds of the bell and responds to the stimulus, sometimes dragging you unwillingly from sleep. A mother can be woken by her small baby crying to be fed at 2 am, while other people in the house—even the baby's own father—will not be disturbed.

Another part of the brain allows us to ignore regular noises, like cars outside or mild rainstorms. In this way even while asleep the brain apparently selects the intake of stimuli and lets us respond to some, but not to all. You can actually exploit or train your mind to some degree: many people say to themselves, 'I must get up early tomorrow' and actually wake up even before the alarm clock rings. Routine can play its part, for you can accustom yourself to waking regularly at 7 or 8 am if this is part of a long standing pattern of living. In the same way, many people always feel hungry at noon or at six.

Orthodox sleep

The activity of the brain during sleep is of course very important when studying dreams. Scientists have found that it is possible to measure brain activity by measuring the electrical impulses constantly given off. These can be registered on a machine called an electro-encephalograph (*cephalos* being the Greek work for 'head'), known as an EEG machine. By attaching electrodes to people's heads in various special spots, an interesting record of brain activity can be obtained. It seems that adults have several levels of sleep. At first, while someone is fully awake but preparing for sleep, a steady wave pattern is detected by the EEG machine. These waves are called 'alpha rhythm'. This is not exactly the same as being wide-awake and fully alert, for if the telephone rings or some other circumstance forces a person to get out of bed, these alpha waves disappear, and a completely different pattern is recorded.

After this first 'alpha rhythm' stage, the brain falls into a second stage of drowsiness, and a pattern of much slower, more irregular waves occurs. Then, finally, the person falls into deep sleep, characterized on the EEG machine by big, deep 'delta' waves, punctuated by small patches of shorter, faster waves, which are termed 'sleep spindles'. This state is known as 'orthodox sleep'.

During sleep, people fluctuate from one level to another, rising up and down through the three main stages in 90-minute cycles. So on average (although this is very rough and does not allow for the immense variety in sleeping habits that has been found), most people have three or four periods of deep, big-wave sleep each night.

Although people tend to think that deeper sleep comes late in the night, there is some evidence to show that the brain derives the most refreshment and benefit from the big-wave levels of sleep that occur in the earlier cycles of the sleep period. It also seems that the first hour or two of sleep goes immediately into the 'delta' wave level. So

Right, above: 'Stop-frame' photography has shown that the body changes position constantly during sleep. Below: The EEG machine records the electric impulses generated by the brain during sleep. Electrodes are also attached to pick up the muscular movement of eyes, throat and heart.

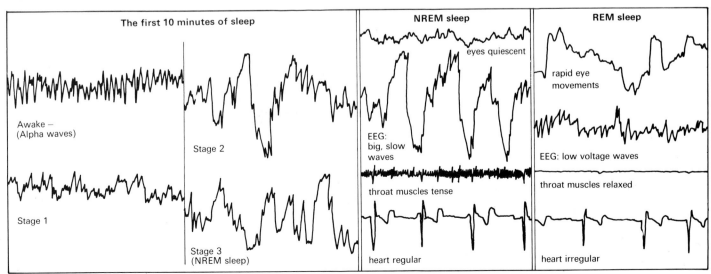

The first 10 minutes of sleep		NREM sleep	REM sleep
Awake — (Alpha waves)	Stage 2	eyes quiescent	rapid eye movements
Stage 1	Stage 3 (NREM sleep)	EEG: big, slow waves	EEG: low voltage waves
		throat muscles tense	throat muscles relaxed
		heart regular	heart irregular

perhaps there is some truth in the saying that sleep before midnight is better than sleep in the early hours—if a person's usual time for going to bed is about 10 pm. But obviously if someone is accustomed to sleeping from midnight until 10 am, he will draw the greatest benefit from his sleep between midnight and 2 am. In the same way, you do not necessarily need double sleep to recuperate from a very late night. In this case, the body simply makes up the lost resting time by going into longer periods of big-wave sleep on the following night. Most people find that a normal period of sleep, that is about 7 to 8 hours, is enough to repair the damage of a late-night party—although it does not take into account other bad effects which might also be present—like alcoholic poisoning from too much drink!

Paradoxical sleep

There is another level of sleep, however, which, because of its 'contradictory' nature, is known as paradoxical sleep. Although the terms 'orthodox' and 'paradoxical' may seem to be an unnecessary complication in the matter of sleeping, it is important to use this distinction. It is easy to make the mistake of thinking that one or the other of the two main stages of sleep is deeper or of better quality. In fact, you should have a fair share of both kinds of sleep for the mind and body to function efficiently.

In the late 1950's, EEG experiments undertaken by Dr. Nathaniel Kleitman achieved a breakthrough in the study of sleep and dreams. It was discovered that people have periods when the wave pattern changes again, this time to a shallow-wave pattern. Their eyes move rapidly about at the same time, up and down and from side to side, although the lids remain closed. You can often notice this kind of reaction in sleeping dogs or cats: their noses or mouths twitch, their tails swish and their eyes seem to be moving, as if looking at something.

This period, called REM (Rapid Eye Movement) sleep, appears to be the time when humans dream most vividly. It would not be true to say it is the only time, for during experiments, people have sometimes been awakened when their eyes were still and their EEG readings showed big-wave sleep, but they were still interrupted in the middle of a dream. However, it does appear that if a person is awakened during REM sleep he remembers his dream most clearly. Georg Mann, a

colleague of Dr. Kleitman's, once described the process as being like a visit to the theatre: the sleeper/dreamer sits in his seat, at first fidgeting expectantly. Then he slowly settles down ('alpha wave' sleep) until he seems spellbound by the action on stage (REM sleep)

'I was at Hawkwell (a house which we had owned in 1949) and my ex-husband was talking about something which was "up the road". In the dream the road was a different road from the one that really ran past the house and I knew we had never been up it. So I asked him suspiciously what he knew about this road. He admitted sheepishly that he had been looking at a new house which was being built up there, which he rather liked. Without actually moving I could see the unfinished house. I asked him what we would get for our house if we sold it. He replied instantly, "£38,000". I thought, "How the hell did he know that?" I knew somehow that the new house was selling for £27,000. So I said, "Why don't we sell this house and move into the new one?" I don't remember any more.'
(NB. The house prices are very specifically in terms of 1970's values, rather than 1949, which seemed to be the period in which the dream took place.)
Librarian, female, 56

---

watching everything with his eyes until the curtain falls. Finally, he shifts again as the play ends ('delta' waves).

Studying people asleep in this way has dispelled one very common misconception: that dreams only take a second or two to occur, even though they seem very long to the dreamer. We now know that dreams take exactly as long as the events would take in real life. People who have dreams or nightmares which force them to wake up at night find that they feel terribly low the next day. They have in fact experienced a loss of satisfying sleeping time.

You may think that the time when you dream is the time when you are most 'relaxed', when the mind has all its defences down so that these strange pictures from your private underworld can well up into your brain—but this is

not the case. During this kind of sleep, the brain is actually sending messages down to the body muscles to stop any action. The muscles of the body are completely relaxed. Remember the description of the man in the theatre, who sits 'spellbound' by the action. The brain prevents us from acting out the events in the dream world. This discovery has helped to explain the horrible sensation when you want to scream but can't or you try to run but remain rooted to the spot, which characterizes vivid dreams and especially nightmares.

Why you need to sleep and dream

How do we know that sleep is vital? This question is easy to answer: it was common experience during World War II when prisoners were tortured by being kept awake, that after a comparatively short period of time, they would suffer serious personality disorders as well as physical discomfort, and some actually died from the effects of sleep deprivation. The fact that the prisoners were forced to stay awake, rather than being allowed even short periods of sleep, was the worst aspect of the torture. Walking about, prolonged shouting sessions, hot and cold showers—any number of activities had to be maintained to keep them going.

The brain must have its regeneration period of sleep and fights very hard to get it. It is perfectly possible to 'drop off' even for a second or two if you are short of sleep. How often has the rocking of a train or the droning voice of a boring public speaker resulted in your nodding off involuntarily?

A regular rhythm or pulse is a great sleep inducer: the cradle and the rocking chair are domestic proof of that. But strangely enough people fall asleep just as readily through something which ought to be stimulating. They sleep in front of the television or at concerts and plays—and then complain bitterly that they cannot sleep in bed! There is also a danger of accidents or damage in jobs which involve driving long distances or operating machines in a factory. Work does not become easier to do because it is repetitive—it is harder to maintain concentration, and people who work in such conditions cannot help but make mistakes or put themselves at risk. It is part of their human make-up.

Learning in bed

The ability of regular rhythm to induce sleep also counters the science-fiction idea of 'learning in one's sleep'. Many people believe that you can learn a foreign language or the lines of a play by playing a repetitive recording through earphones while you are asleep. It seems unlikely that this could ever happen, since the process of sleep stops the stimulation of the 'wakeful' part of the brain which is normally the area capable of learning and memorizing new information. In fact you are much more likely to be woken up by a recording, just as you would by the telephone or alarm clock.

However, the best time to learn in bed is for a short period when 'alpha rhythms' are present. This is when the body is relaxed ready for sleep but still awake mentally. Perhaps this accounts for the pleasantness of reading in bed—quite complicated material can be well absorbed at this time of night. But don't overdo it—if you're trying to cram for exams or finish vital work for the next day, you'll do more damage by not having enough sleep than forcing yourself to stay awake and learn!

Sleep is vital, in both its orthodox and paradoxical forms, and it follows that dreaming is all important as well. But don't worry if you think you never dream. You do—but you may never *remember* them on waking.

Scientific experiments have shown that if a person is deprived of sleep altogether, then his first night's sleep afterwards will be spent in a greater proportion of orthodox, deep-wave sleep than usual. But after that, on the second or third night, he will make up the paradoxical sleep of vivid dreaming that he has missed. This suggests that both kinds of sleep are equally necessary and work in different ways for our benefit. It might simply be habit to have these two kinds of sleep, but it is also possible that orthodox sleep feeds our body, while paradoxical sleep feeds our mind or brain.

Bad sleepers

It is quite possible that someone who complains of being a 'bad sleeper' might be expecting too much and might be getting quite enough sleep for his own needs. Older people definitely need less sleep—the cells of their bodies and brain are not being renewed at the same rate as a growing child. Remember also that short snatches of sleep—even seconds long—can fall on people, so that in an apparently sleepless night, you can never really be certain that you didn't 'drop off' for a moment. People who sleep badly probably come straight up into full consciousness from deep-

wave sleep more often than 'good' sleepers, who usually have a period of doziness before awakening fully. In other words, bad sleepers remember periods of wakefulness more vividly than other people and consequently believe that they hardly sleep at all.

Sleeping pills

People often believe that sleeping pills will help them to sleep 'well', especially if they are plagued by distressing insomnia. However, there is a great danger in their use, especially the barbiturates. Many psychologists have produced evidence that if you take sleeping pills, you do not get the normal amount of paradoxical sleep—the sleep of vivid dreams and mental regeneration. People frequently find that even though they take sleeping pills, they do not wake up feeling refreshed—a complaint that can now be explained partly by the need for two kinds of sleep.

It may be a temporary relief from the day's worries to force the mind into

Gustav Doré's 'The Exercise Yard' conveys the despair of sleeplessness. Luckily the body has an invincible capacity for snatching sleep.

oblivion with barbiturates. But in the long run, this is only evading the issue. You are actively preventing your mind from facing up to your life-situation and possibly from helping you to understand yourself, so that whatever you are doing can be sorted out. Worse still, as the body really dislikes these drugs, it will make strenuous efforts to overcome their effect. This is what happens when the effect of the drug begins to 'wear off'. It is not uncommon for people to experience far worse sleeplessness and much more intense 'imaginings in the night' than if they had not embarked on pill-taking in the first place.

Sleeping pills can be just as habit forming as alcohol and can have just as serious results. If people would think of them as dangerous, perhaps they would not damage themselves by relying on them habitually.

An interesting sidelight to the problem of drugs can be seen in the immense reaction that many individuals experience after an operation under full anaesthetic. An anaesthetic immobilizes the body, cutting out physical pain and conscious awareness. However, it could be that part of the brain does register what is going on, which is why anaesthetics can give a nastier shock to the system than the surgery performed under it. Even a minor event like having tonsils removed can bring about very vivid dreams for days or weeks afterwards. If one isolated, safely supervised event can have such marked repercussions on the brain, no wonder that prolonged pill-taking is so

destructive, even if at first it seems a dull, wonderful relief.

No-one would suggest, however, that prolonged periods of sleeplessness should be ignored, and no doctor would discuss them as mere complaining. Severe insomnia can be successfully treated—but not merely by popping in a pill every night year after year.

Sleepwalking

Sleepwalking is a severe form of night disturbance, often incorrectly associated with insomnia. It is, on the contrary, linked with the deep orthodox sleep where no eye movements occur. Sleepwalkers are not acting out the

events of their dreams, but the activity seems to indicate that there is some form of mental activity going on in orthodox sleep. People have reported dreams when awakened during this stage, but they are generally less vivid and more difficult to remember for any length of time. The exact nature of the mind's activity during sleepwalking is still a mystery, but it may indicate emotional disturbance. In a child it appears most commonly to be a sign of anxiety or upset, so a doctor should be consulted if it persists. The one excep-

Children are especially prone to visions of 'bogey men' during the dozey phase before sleep.

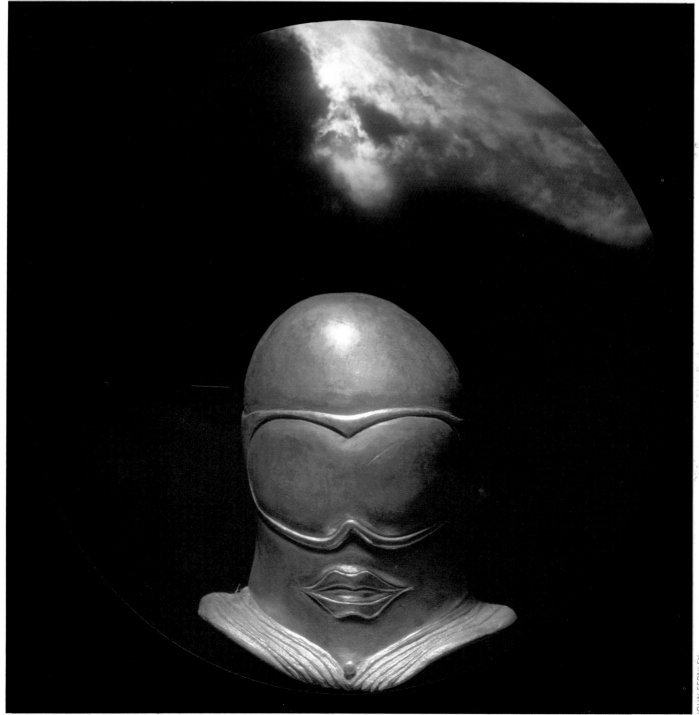

tion to this advice would be if the family had a long history of sleepwalking—for some reason the phenomenon is quite often hereditary.

Things that go bump in the night!

One of the most familiar and easily explicable forms of night disturbance is found during the 'dozey' phase, which takes place just before deep sleep and also just before normal awakening (as opposed to a sharp jolt into alertness). The commonest effect is to imagine that you are falling or that the whole bed is floating. It is also well-known to have a quick imagining of a car crash and literally to jump or start violently at the moment of impact. For children this is the time when 'bogeymen' stand at the foot of the bed, or eerie faces float before the closed eyes. One man remembers vividly that a head made of black and yellow houndstooth check tweed would hover at the end of his bed almost every night at one period of his childhood! Everyone knows the dread of seeing a menacing stranger in the room—it turns out to be the same old dressing gown on the back of the door. The scientific name for an experience of this sort is a 'hypnagogic' dream, a word which only signifies the time when these visions appear, which is in the period leading towards sleep.

All this activity of the brain is reflected in the wave patterns taken from sleepers wired to an EEG machine. Falling asleep is not a steady flow downwards into deep relaxation, but the 'alpha waves' of drowsiness—although regular —rise and fall on a general downward path. It is like watching the flames of a dying fire: they fade steadily, but there can occasionally be a little burst of life.

Dreams and your body

The idea of linking bodily states with the content of dreams is one that has excited great interest for many years. At one time it was thought that dreams were merely the result of eating a heavy meal too late at night. Certain foodstuffs, such as cheese, were supposed to have a particularly strong effect on people, causing vivid dreams. Any form of physical imbalance, such as the discomfort caused to the stomach from over-eating or indigestion, can cause dreaming, but nevertheless does not account for the extraordinary pictures created in our dreams. If food was the reason for a dream, as opposed to one possible cause, people eating cheese would all have exactly the same

cheesey dream—but they don't. However, certain patterns can be noted in the way the body adjusts to outside stimuli. If someone falls asleep resting uncomfortably on an arm, he is quite likely to have a dream involving something unpleasant happening to that limb, such as paralysis or being wounded. But as dreams tend to draw attention to something we should recognize about ourselves, it would be quite feasible that the mind could choose this bizarre way of letting the sleeper know about the discomfort—forcing him to wake up or at least turn over.

In one series of experiments, Calvin Hall, the American researcher, has proved this kind of influence on dreams by placing a waxed candle in a dreamer's hands on two occasions. The first time, the man dreamed he was playing golf, and the second time, he imagined he was lifting weights in a gymnasium! Hearing a tap dripping is a familiar example which often transforms itself in dreams into something like rain, tears, or pouring wine. Sleeping on one's back can cause pressure on the spinal cord and some dreams re-create the pain in a nightmare.

Nightmares

Nightmares are dreams which create a picture or feeling which is so terrifying or disturbing that it wakes you up. Some scientists believe that certain body functions are behind them. Small children find the emotions of rage or hatred so strange and overpowering that at night they re-create them as a particularly forceful dream-picture. This idea is reinforced by the fact that nightmares start in children just about the age when they develop an understanding of good and bad behaviour. So, saying to a 4 or 5 year old, 'You'll really get it if you pinch Suzy again' impresses on the child a sense that many of its natural feelings are bad and dangerous. Consequently he has nightmares in which he realizes the awful consequences of letting 'naughtiness' get out of hand. In older people nightmares can often be a repeat of these childhood fears and may indicate that there is a problem still unsolved in the person's character.

This idea is taken further by other psychologists who believe that people often have nightmares as a result of half-understood physical sensations. Girls in their teens, waking up to the idea of sex, often have very intense dreams which are representations of their emerging sexual drive. What you do not understand often frightens you

—and so the dream becomes a nightmare, with a 'big black thing' chasing you and your legs refusing to move. Dreams of falling from high places can be quite terrifying as well—but they can also occur with no feeling of fear at all! Some of the most disturbing nightmares that adults experience are caused by anxiety. As often as not the events of the dream may seem inocuous enough, but the atmosphere of fear, disgust, anger, sorrow or bewilderment will be the dominant feeling, enough to wake you and leave you feeling disturbed and agitated for some time afterwards.

Dreams and illness

There is an extension to the physiological aspect of dream-making that occurs rarely, but cannot be overlooked. It has been known for someone to dream of being seriously ill, in a very specific way, such as dreaming of suffocation, when in reality the dreamer is a victim of asthma. There are also notable instances of precognitive dreams about illness, in which people have dreamed of having a heart attack or a brain tumour several months before the conditions have actually been diagnosed.

Many people dream about things of which they are afraid or worried, so in most cases a dream about illness will have this simple cause behind it. It expresses the worst fears of the dreamer, so that the problem of anxiety is brought into the open. In rare cases, it could be that the heart trouble or other disorder is present in some slight form, and this registers on the unconscious mind before the conscious one, producing a dream-picture of the trouble. No one should believe that 'bad' news in a dream will necessarily come true: a dream about cancer probably indicates that you have a real anxiety about this illness and the best way to cure that is to have regular checks, as advised by most doctors.

Whatever the factors which cause a dream—outside noises, inside stomach grumblings, or imagined fears—the pictures which are presented to a dreamer are unique, private and endlessly varied. The poet Keats once described sleep as a 'soft embalmer of the still midnight', and asked,
'Save me from curious Conscience, that still lords
Its strength for darkness, burrowing like a mole'.
But research has shown that sleep, while essential and refreshing, still allows the burrowing to continue for our own good.

Dreams without Freud

Dream interpretation is not new; it is one of the oldest and most widespread arts. Ever since man has been capable of coherent communication he has been fascinated by the meaning of the strange frightening and inconsequential meanderings of the unconscious.

The Mesopotamian theory

Of the early civilizations known to man, Mesopotamia developed the most comprehensive and sophisticated explanation for dreams and their language. The emphasis laid on sex by Freud's theories is not as revolutionary as you might think. In ancient texts written by the Babylonians and Assyrians, some dating back as far as 5000 BC, a large amount of space is devoted to explanations of sexual images in dreams.

If a man dreamed that his urine streamed out directly against a wall and spread in the street, then he would have many children. Dreams of flying, which Freud interpreted as symbolic of sexual pleasure, were a subject of great interest to the Mesopotamians. They wrote long books on the various meanings, but most agreed that flight signified danger or death.

These early books about dreams contain many images and symbols of everyday actions, especially eating and drinking, and deal with animals such as donkeys, horses, goats and cats. The Mesopotamians believed that dreams came from evil spirits or demons and that they were like spells, bound to come true unless the dreamer did something to avert them.

The Babylonians had a goddess of dreams, Mamu, to whom they prayed and whose priests performed rituals to stop dreams from being fulfilled.

Nebuchadnezzar's dream

In the Bible, the Babylonian king Nebuchadnezzar dreamed of a strong flourishing tree, cursed by a 'holy one', which turned into a withered stump. The Hebrew prophet Daniel, who was renowned as a dream interpreter, told the King that the image forecast madness. The Bible relates that one year later, Nebuchadnezzar did indeed become insane, 'till his hairs were grown like eagles' feathers, and his nails like birds' claws'. This can be seen either as an example of an evil spirit's dream come true, as the Babylonians would have believed, or as showing that Nebuchadnezzar felt within himself a premonition of his own illness and downfall. Certainly the dream is a good example of the Jungian view that all images are reflections of the self: the tree was the king's mind.

Dreams of the Egyptian dynasties

Egyptian relics of dream books show that their beliefs were quite similar to those of the Babylonians and Assyrians, although they do not date back as far in time—to about 3000 BC. They too were concerned with sexual dreams, and incest and bestiality crop up very often. No one is certain whether this means that people really did make love to their close relatives or to animals, or simply had fantasies about it. The Egyptians subscribed to the theory that dreams come from evil spirits who had to be appeased in some way. However, there were dreams from good spirits, too.

Pharoah's dream

The Old Testament is full of stories about dreams, the best-known being those told by the Pharoah to Joseph. Seven well-fed cattle came out of a river to feed in a meadow, followed by seven lean ones, who then ate the fat cattle. On the following night, Pharoah dreamed of seven good ears of corn that were eaten by seven thin, blasted ears. Joseph interpreted these dreams correctly as a forecast of seven years of plenty to be followed by seven of famine. Notice how the dreams go over the same ground on two consecutive nights, using different images to convey the same message. This trick is still recognized in modern theories as a part of the dream language.

Dream temples—Epyptian style

The Egyptian word for dreaming means the same as 'to keep awake' and shows that they connected dreams with some great state of knowing or seeing things in the dark. So deep was their faith in dream messages that they built temples to which they would go to pray for helpful dreams. Skilled dream-interpreters were on hand to explain the contents next day. If a revealing dream would not come, then there were a host of spells and incantations to make one appear. One remedy was to 'take a cat, black all over, which has been killed; prepare a writing tablet and write with a solution of myrrh the spell and its destination and put it into the mouth of the cat'.

Dreams in ancient Asia

The ancient Chinese and Indian people went much further with their studies of dreams. They did not simply work out lists of what certain images in dreams meant, like the Mesopotamians and Egyptians had done, and they modified the idea that dreams come from outside forces, from good or bad spirits.

The ancient Chinese made a distinction between the different levels of consciousness long before western psychologists began to discuss its existence. They accepted that dreams are produced by the unconscious mind and wrote many books studying the different symbols used in dreams, including the I Ching which is arousing great interest nowadays among people interested in the workings of the mind. Its approach seems to many to have a deeper insight into the subject than many books of western philosophy.

The Chinese rationalization

Chinese writers tried to work out some overall reason for dreams, drawing on astrology and taking note of the time, season and bodily condition of the dreamer. Dreams were classified into several types: ordinary, terrifying, thoughtful, waking, joyful and fearful. (These were mentioned in a book written around 500 BC: the Lio-tzu). Like many ancient peoples, the Chinese believed that in sleep, a part of the body is able to wander, to experience dreams, and that great care must be taken not to rouse the sleeper too suddenly, before he has time to return to himself. Nowadays this idea is still given credence by spiritualists and others who believe in 'astral projection', the idea that everyone has an 'astral body' capable of leaving the physical one and wandering at will, usually during sleep.

This quaint medieval view of Nebuchadnezzar's dream shows the effects of his later madness. His dream was a classic example of the subconscious revealing death or a future illness.

Indian understanding

The idea of different states in the body intrigued the Indians, who also developed a subtle understanding of different levels of consciousness. They thought there were four states: waking, dreaming, dreamless sleep, and a fourth, which is a mystical union with the god Brahmin. It is extraordinary to think that several centuries before Christ, the notion of distinction between different types of sleep was already being considered, although it

has taken years for modern scientific research to confirm this with EEG machine experiments.

One of the earliest Indian dream books is contained in the Atharva Veda, an old collection of writings dating from around 1500-1000 BC. Among its many fascinating ideas is the suggestion that if a man has a series of dreams, only the last should be considered important. This ties in neatly with the modern concept that several dreams work through a problem in different ways until they find a solution. The

Indian theory suggests that they realized that dreams could have a purpose.

They also accepted two kinds of imagery in dreams: those relating to common experience and those having a more general wide symbolism. This is a feature of modern understanding that finds echoes in the early writings. Images which Freud took to be sexual—swords, axes, flags—were taken to mean happiness. Symbols such as the sun or moon falling from the sky or dreams involving the sea or mountains suggested messages of a different kind,

usually dangerous or fearful. This is rather like Jung's explanation of archetypal images, which people everywhere can recognize, whatever their own personal experience. Basic emotions are expressed through them.

Perhaps even more remarkable insight is found in these early Hindu writings in the practice of looking at the temperament or character of the dreamer. This was only hinted: the main drift of ancient Indian belief was to think of some mysterious 'other force' at work, but nevertheless, even a suggestion that someone's personality is related to his dreams is a very modern idea.

The Classical idea

Fundamentally, the eastern religions of Hinduism and Buddhism are much more contemplative than those of the western world, so perhaps the emphasis on states of mind is understandable. In comparison, the classical worlds of Greece and Rome used dreams more as signs about how to act or what was going to happen. Famous writers and poets such as Homer give many instances of people prompted to action because of some message from a god revealed in a dream.

Dream temples, Greek style
The hero Achilles in the story of the fall of Troy, the Iliad, believes that the god Zeus will aid the Greeks with advice revealed in a dream. So widespread was this view that the Greeks took up the Egyptian idea of building temples where people could go to sleep, to dream and to have a 'divine' message descend on them.

The temples were dedicated to Aesculapius, the Greek god of healing, for it was also believed that medical cures could be achieved through dreams. A dream could specify the right kind of treatment, besides revealing to someone a proper course of action. Hippocrates, (a medical man from whom we still have the 'Hippocratic oath' which doctors are supposed to swear) wrote a book about dreams, one of the few that have survived from the classical era.

The Hippocratic theory
Hippocrates explains in great detail a belief shared by the Greek people with other parts of the early world. Everything that happens to a human being, in sickness or in dreams for instance, is a reflection of some larger state of affairs in the universe. A man is controlled by the powers that cause the sun and moon to shine or the earth to bear crops, and so an event like an eclipse or a flood has a terrifying effect. It also explains why the idea of some outside power or god speaking in dreams would have been credible.

The Platonic theory
Not all Greek thinkers shared this view. Plato developed an explanation of dreams that bears some resemblance to Freud's line of thought. At night, he said, we have a 'wild beast' roaming around inside us, while reason sleeps. The passions in us which drive us to commit murder, sacrilege or incest can come out in dreams. Freud also narrowed down the kind of drives that make us dream to those of sex and power. There is a noticeable link in his theory of the conscious and the unconscious with Plato's idea of reason being asleep while the wild beast roams.

Dreams and Romans

The Romans held to most of the views of the Greeks and were prompted by their dream images to do things with just as much sincerity. Hannibal crossed the Alps after being encouraged in a dream, and Julius Caesar came to power in the same way. When returning to Rome at the head of his army, he dreamed one night of sleeping with his mother. This he took as a sign of 'entering the mother land' and promptly crossed the Rubicon into Roman territory with his troops. This entry was forbidden unless a general disbanded his forces first and was symbolic of seizing the power of the empire.

Artemidorus:
linking past and present
The most famous of all books about dreams to come out of the classical world was written by Artemidorus of Daldis in the second century AD. Throughout his life, he gathered together a vast store of ancient documents relating to dreams in order to write a major study of the subject. He actually used material from the great library of the Babylonian king, Asurnasi at Nineveh. In this way, a clear tradition of dream interpretation survived from the earliest days of civilization to the first centuries of the Christian era. Perhaps these strange connections account for the disrepute which fell on Artemidorus: he was taken up by magicians and quacks seeking to prove some mystical line of authority back to ancient prophets and seers. But if all this is left aside, the real value of Artemidorus' work is immense. He was the first person to see clearly that dreams are made up of a number of images, strung together in a sequence. He believed it was very important to study the whole dream and to see the images in their setting. This has long since been accepted as an essential method for worthwhile understanding of dreams. Second, Artemidorus said that it was always necessary to have a good knowledge of a dreamer's personality and his life situation—and that is exactly what modern psychoanalysts try to discover and what you should apply to the interpretation of your own dreams.

'I was riding down the road on a bicycle and somebody started following me, also on a bicycle. He started terrorizing me — I was terribly frightened and I kept trying to get help, but I could not speak or shout. All the time my hands kept getting caught in the spokes of the bicycle wheel.
I got to a phone booth and two traffic wardens walked by laughing and talking and they saw me struggling and screaming trying to get into this telephone booth but I could not actually get anything out of my throat at all, and they obviously were thinking "How cute, this young couple you know, having a lark", and that frightened me even more. Eventually I got in the phone booth and I tried to telephone Mike, my husband, to save me, and then I realized that he was the one who was terrorizing me at the same time. Eventually I actually managed to get the words out and I actually shot up in bed screaming for help.'
Picture researcher, 25, female

There is more than a grain of truth in another suggestion from Artemidorus: many dream images have a strong sexual element, he said. The plough in the furrow, the horse and carriage and the granary store were all studied in what we now call 'Freudian' terms. He also commented, 'a mirror means a woman to a man and a man to a woman', which neatly expresses the same idea as Jung's description of the Animus and Anima. These two are our sexual opposites, acting as an expression of our aggressive, masculine nature or passive, more feminine side.

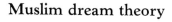

Muslim dream theory

Dream interpretation began to go out of favour in Europe once the magical associations surrounding Artemidorus' theories became known. Only the non-Christians, the Muslim Arabs, continued to be fascinated by it.

They studied all the writers from classical times and from the far eastern part of their empire, where information filtered through from China and the Indian sub-continent. Subtle and mysterious explanations were put forward, and hundreds of books, from dictionaries and encyclopedias to religious treatises and magical poems, were written by Arab scholars.

Mahomet's explanation of faith

Mahomet, the founder of Islam, used dreams as a way of explaining the faith. He relates in the Koran a dream in which the angel Gabriel takes him on a journey through the night, riding a silvery grey mare, all the way to Jerusalem and then up to heaven. He meets Adam, the four Apostles, Jesus and finally sees the Garden of Delights. He meets God, who gives him instructions for his people about how many times a day his people should say their prayers. Then the beautiful grey mare

flies through the dark sky, back to the spot on earth where he had fallen asleep.

Although there were many knowledgeable dream interpreters, the Muslims tended to explain dreams in a way that fitted in well with their religious beliefs. And there are some amazing insights in Arabic works:

'He whose soul is pure is never deceived by his dreams, whereas he whose soul is blemished is continually deluded'.

There also was an attempt to understand symbols, especially those which we now consider to be Jungian archetypes. But in the end, the skill was limited by the main purpose, that of explaining people's thoughts in terms of the rules of the Islamic faith.

Dreams and Christianity

In the Christian world, dreams fared even worse. The Church frowned on 'interpreting', believing it was involved with sorcery and black magic. It only allowed the possibility that dreams could be divinely inspired. It is very interesting to see that all the dreams reported by religious figures in the New Testament and in early Christianity do not require any interpreting at all. They are nearly always straightforward mes-

Mahomet used his dream of a journey to heaven on a silvery grey mare to inspire faith, but it could be seen as an expression of his own ambitions as a spiritual leader.

sages of encouragement from God. There was no thought of foretelling a man's future, for that was in God's hands.

Francis of Assisi

St. Francis of Assisi recorded many dreams which he had at important moments in his life, all of which gave him the strength to carry on in his life of poverty and to continue the establishment of his order of Franciscan monks. One striking image came to him just before a very difficult interview with Pope Innocent III. He saw a tall tree with wide, thick branches before him. As he looked at it in admiration, he felt himself growing and growing until he was the same height as the tree. He touched it with his hand and it gently gave way, bending down at his touch. St. Francis saw this as a sign from God that the Catholic Pope would give way and accept his ideas. (Notice how both St. Francis and King Nebuchadnezzar took the world-wide symbol of a tree to express their wishes and fears.)

Famous precognitive dreams

This limitation on dream interpretation continued for many centuries, and only in the last hundred years have people begun to look at dreams from the point of view of the personality. The other aspect of their contents that fascinated thinkers was the occurrence of dreams that seemed to foretell the future.

Nearly all biographies of famous people contain such startling incidents.

Francis Bacon, Elizabethan writer and scientist was staying in Paris while his father was lying seriously ill in London, England. One night when his father was near death, Bacon dreamed of his family home in the country, and that it was plastered with 'black mortar'. This led him to believe that there could be some form of telepathic communication between blood relatives.

Oliver Cromwell when a young man had a dream in which a huge female figure drew back the curtains round his bed and told him that one day he would be the greatest man in England. Cromwell especially noted later that no mention had been made of the word, king. (The female figure could be interpreted as the Jungian concept of the anima: while Cromwell's remark could be a good example of 'secondary revision' as Freud would say – adding in a conscious detail to an unconscious experience.)

THE MANSELL COLLECTION

Queen Marie Antoinette, overthrown and imprisoned by the French revolutionaries, had a dream of a glowing red sun rising above a column, like a temple pillar. Suddenly the column cracked in half and fell to the ground. Her image has been understood to represent the fall of a powerful figure.

Shelley had a dream no less than a fortnight before he drowned in the Mediterranean, sailing from Leghorn, in which friends came into his bedroom, seriously wounded and bloodstained, with staring faces, warning him that the house was being flooded by the sea. He also dreamed in the same moment of strangling his friend, Williams, who did indeed drown with him.

Charles Dickens had a dream in which he saw a lady in a red shawl with her back towards him. She turned round and introduced herself with the words 'I am Miss Napier'. Dickens had no idea who this person was, but the very next night, after giving one of his famous readings, some friends came backstage, bringing with them the selfsame woman, and introducing her as 'Miss Napier' in real life.

THE MANSELL COLLECTION

Bismarck, the iron ruler of nineteenth century Germany, dreamed of the rise to power of Prussia over the other German states. This actually came true and was one cause of the First World War.

THE MANSELL COLLECTION

Abraham Lincoln dreamed of his own violent death, with his body lying in state on a catafalque.

PAUL POPPER LTD

Adolf Hitler had a most extraordinary dream as a young man during the First World War. He was a member of the German Infantry and found himself in the trenches on the French front. One night, he dreamed of being buried beneath an avalanche of earth and molten iron and of being severely wounded. He woke up and felt compelled to leave the trench in spite of warnings from his comrades. No sooner had he started to scramble away from the dug-out than a fearful explosion thudded behind him. Hitler turned back to see the trench completely collapsed and all the soldiers dying under a mass of earth and hot metal. It has been said that the event encouraged Hitler to believe that he could not fail in his plan to dominate Europe.

Nowadays, a large part of dream research is directed into this area of dreams which foresee. Sometimes of course it can be argued that they are merely another version of wish-fulfilling or problem-solving dreams. Both Marie Antoinette and Bismarck might be expected to have such dreams, given the circumstances of their lives. But not all, certainly not Hitler's dream, could be brushed off in this way.

Lord Tennyson dreamed of Prince Albert coming to see him and kissing him on the cheek. 'Very kind but very German' he said to himself in the dream. The very next day, he got a letter from Windsor Castle informing him that he was to be Poet Laureate.

The Duke of Portland, who was involved in arranging the Coronation of Edward VII, had a dream that the king's coach got stuck in the Arch at Horse Guards on its way to Westminster Abbey. Although the State Coach had been used before, he insisted on the arch and the coach being measured, and found that the top of the coach was too high to pass under the arch. Since its last appearance, the road surface had been raised due to repair work, and everyone had overlooked the fact.

Dreams in primitive cultures

These are the traditional views and mysteries of dream history. Now that you have seen how many ideas date back to the earliest civilizations, you will not be surprised to learn that psychologists have gathered some very useful information in recent years from looking at present-day primitive tribes, some nearly extinct. The data collected can yield valuable comparisons and sidelights on the way that all minds work, primitive or sophisticated, and shows how widespread and fundamental certain ideas are.

The Siriono of the Amazon
Looking at tribes all over the world has proved that people dream to a large extent about the everyday facts of their lives, wherever they are. We might have dreams situated in houses and motor cars, whereas the Siriono natives of the Amazon in South America dream about hunting in the jungle. Just as we use the image of the car to suggest other things besides transport, (mechanical emotions, sexual drive and so on) so the Siriono people dream about hunting, even when they are not hungry. They turn hunting into an image to suggest other things. This leads to the conclusion that all human beings use typical parts of their living pattern to make images in their dream world.

The Sioux Indians
Many discoveries about so-called primitive people suggest that perhaps they have better ways of living than we do ourselves! The North American Sioux Indians, for example, dealt very kindly with the misfits of their society. They somehow fitted them in, instead of shutting them away in a kind of institution. They did not regard the criminal, the insane or inadequate as shameful or stupid. They put all the blame on evil spirits who had infected the dream world of these poor people and treated them as best they could. In a way, this recognizes that people have an unconscious part to their minds that produces drives without respect to the conscious part. Other tribes seem to have understood this too, although it took western civilization many centuries to come to the same conclusion through psychology.

The Iroquois Indians
The Iroquois Indians worked out a theory that dreams may say one thing

In primitive societies, the barrier between the world of dreams and ordinary daily experience is not so sharply defined. The Sioux bear dance was a symbolic enactment of the roles of hunter and hunted.

THE MANSELL COLLECTION

but mean another, and they devised special techniques to help people discover the true meaning. The Iroquois used a method rather like that suggested earlier of writing down or recording all the thoughts that spring to mind in association with a dream image to build up some impression of what it represents.

Once the Iroquois dreamer had a clear idea of what wish was being expressed or what problem was being confronted, then the Indians would 'make it come true' by acting it out, either in reality by staging an argument or in a ritualistic way. More developed societies also have ways of releasing some urges as a ritual — all the howling and shouting at a football game could be viewed as a fairly healthy way to express aggression!

The Hurons

The Huron Indians had a theory which has quite noticeable resemblances with modern ideas about dreams. Like many primitive cultures, these Indians believed that the 'voice' of the dream world was a guardian spirit, which gave revelatory messages, but in disguised form. These could be warnings about enemies, disclosures of special cures for diseases or good advice about the best places to go hunting. Especially interesting is the belief that this 'spirit-voice' could reveal the hidden wishes of the scul – rather like the Freudian idea that dreams are expressions of unconscious urges or wishes. The Hurons came even closer to modern thought when they suggested that perhaps the 'spirit' or 'soul' inside is made happy or satisfied by expressing its desire in dream form. This led them to wonder whether in fact physical illness or emotional upset is caused by the 'spirit' rebelling because its desires are not recognized – not far off present-day thinking about psychosomatic illness.

The Diegueno Indians

These Indians of Southern California have been studied with great interest because they devised a technique of psychotherapy through dreams – a development not found very often among primitive people. The 'treatment' was confined to people who were suffering from a particular type of obsession or fantasy. This was sexual and consisted of excessive dreaming on the subject, in mild form, or hallucinations, when it was considered serious. These visions would be of a 'spirit-lover' plaguing the sufferer. The treat-

ment would be to have a lengthy conversation with a shaman or magic man, who encouraged the patient to confess his fantasies and discuss why they are so absorbing. The shaman declares that he might as well tell all, because he knows all about it anyway, through his magic powers. He might also recommend the sufferer to go on a special healthful diet – or get married! But the significant aspect of this Diegueno custom is that the remedy takes the form of a consultation – a talking-out with an expert – much the same as a modern analyst works. In most primitive groups, remedies are usually more physical: people 'act out' the dream or dance away the affliction.

Two recurring dreams:
'I'm in some play or other, but I've been idle about learning my lines. I've lost my script so I search high and low, but I can't find it and no one else will lend me one. Then it's time to go on stage, and I still don't know my lines.'
Librarian, female, 56

'I kept dreaming that I was going down a spiral staircase — like in a castle or church tower, As I went down it got narrower and narrower until I was stuck with my shoulders above and my legs round the corner below!'
Housewife, 30

The Ashanti People

The foregoing examples concern American people, but of course, African studies have come up with equally varied and surprising facts. These too help to build up some basic conclusions about the nature of dreaming, worldwide. The Ashanti of West Africa, for example, had also caught hold of the idea that dreams can mean exactly the opposite of their apparent content, just as Freud has pointed out in his Interpretation of Dreams.

To give an example: someone may dream that a hunter kills an elephant. The Ashanti method would be to look beyond the immediate images and find the real answer by association of ideas. The elephant is the most powerful animal of the jungle, so he must represent a king or chief. The Ashanti would

say therefore that the dream is a warning that a chief will die in the near future. A similar explanation is given for a dream of a house without a roof. This is a symbol foretelling death because for the Ashanti, spirit people live in a world of roofless dwellings.

The Ashanti also share the common idea that the 'voice' of a man's dream is a spirit, and they believe that it can be someone's ancestor speaking. It is a widespread notion, and takes many forms. With the Ashanti, the ancestor often appears in dreams in animal shape. Some anthropologists have been led by this idea into linking dreams of ancestors with totem worship. This is simply another way of saying that primitive people maintain a strong sense of their tradition and identity by worshipping their ancestors and by personifying them as animal or half-imaginary beings. This sometimes involves making actual totem images of them, which are respected and revered by the whole tribe.

Totems and dreams

There are many different theories about what totems are, but the basic idea explained above is common to several of them. A totem acts as a symbol of the group or tribal identity and is often imbued with magical or beneficial powers. This story from a Canadian tribe reveals how totems work for primitive people: A man went out hunting and met a black bear who took him home and taught him many things. After a long stay with the bear the man returned home. At first he looked and acted so like a bear that everyone was afraid of him, but someone rubbed him with magical herbs and he became a man again. After that, whenever he went hunting, the bear helped him catch his quarry. The man built a home and painted a bear on it and his sister made a blanket with a bear design too. Then all the descendants of his sister used the bear crest and were always known as the bear clan.

Such legends occur all over the world and very often the origin of the totem comes from a dream picture. Totems can be personal too: among some Australian aborigines, witch doctors adopt a special totem after dreaming of a particular thing, such as a lizard or a kangaroo. A rather attractive custom from the Dyaks of Borneo illustrates

The most striking characteristic in dreaming among African cultures such as the Ashanti is their belief that dreams are as real as waking experience.

how far and wide this dream influence extends: if a man dreams that something of value is given to him, then when he wakes, he picks up the first curious object he sees – perhaps a shiny stone on the ground. He takes it home and hangs it over his bed, and when he next goes to sleep, he addresses it and says he wants a dream with good pictures about some matter or business which is important to him at the time. If he has such a dream he keeps the object and it becomes valuable to him, but if the dream is unhelpful he throws it away and waits for another such opportunity.

Dreams directing reality

It is quite common among primitive people for special talents or careers to be marked out by a dream experience. Among the Blackfoot Indians of North America for instance a man became a medicine man after he had had a series of dreams in which a dead relative came to him and gave him detailed instructions on how to work cures or cast spells. In many tribes, a young man who intends to become a priest can only do so if he has a dream of making contact with a god first. This is a reminder of the Old Testament story of Samuel, who as a child heard a voice in the night and thought it was his priest, Eli. But the priest, who had been sound asleep, realized that the boy had heard the voice of God.

General conclusions

It seems that primitive people have two kinds of dreams: those that relate to their own personal situation and which come to them quite spontaneously, or those that are more important, containing messages or visions about the whole life of the tribe, its identity and importance. This second kind is sometimes called a 'culture' dream and is obviously considered valuable. In many tribes, special customs exist to induce this kind of dream. They help to keep the group sense of security and well-being, or they can result from the dreamer's wish to be blessed by his ancestors or receive good omens from the 'spirit' of the tribe. In our own culture, we have examples of this kind of dreaming, like Joseph's dreams, and their importance in Bible history.

Dreams are used by primitive people for a number of other social functions, like choosing a person's career or guiding his work. In fact, primitive people use dreams in ways not far removed from those which present-day interpreters suggest they are considered for problem-solving and help towards better self-understanding.

'True' dreaming

The most general belief that characterizes primitive people's dreaming life is that at times they can be just as real and 'truthful' as everyday life. There are endless variations on this theme. If an Ashanti dreams of adultery then this

> "I'm in London and for some time without explanation, the streets have been getting sinister splits in them and steam and smoke start oozing out. Men with wheelbarrows of tar keep trying to fill the cracks. Nobody talks about it but every time you go past a street that's been newly tarred, you know that's another one where the steam has got through.
> I go to visit a friend on the other side of London, in a room with a few large plants, a hickory floor, Bauhaus furniture. We decide we had better get out of London. We run as fast as we can go to Victoria Station. There's a bus like an airport bus, with no seats in it, only some ill-fitting, garishly patterned carpet. A thick, bull-necked man with an SS armband comes up and says "You haven't been members of the Party. You can't leave London."
> We start running, running back to my home, and everywhere the streets are cracking open, melting, boiling, and the smoke is so thick it's dark as night. We rush into a black marbled doorway where there are electric lights and luscious green plants with red and orange veins.
> Then the lights go out and flames start creeping out of the crevasses."
> Magazine editor, 36.

results in his paying a fine just as if he had committed the act. The Didinga people of the south-east Sudan had the custom that if a man dreamed of another as a victim of witchcraft, then the dreamer had to go and see him the very next morning and avert the evil by a series of elaborate ritual acts. If a member of the Dyaks of Borneo dreams of falling into water, he believes that this has actually happened to his spirit and so has to summon a shaman or priest-figure. The shaman 'fishes' for the lost spirit in a basin of water with a little hand net until he catches it and returns it safely to its owner. A tribe in Brazil called the Bororo once deserted a whole village in a panic because one of them dreamed that he saw enemies approaching on the attack. But perhaps the most famous anecdote on this subject comes from the distinguished pioneer scholar in anthropology, Levy-Bruhl, who wrote how a chief in equatorial Africa had a dream that he travelled to Portugal and England. When he got up the next day he put on European clothing and announced his journey to his friends, who all gathered round and congratulated him on his wonderful luck!

The power of dreams

Primitive people may use dreams to predict the future or direct the actions of the tribe or clan. Or they can use dreams to sort out some personality problem, or even a physical illness. The interest for us lies in seeing how primitive people believe so absolutely in the power of dreams. It is easy to see that if a young man dreams that he is in contact with a god, for instance, and accepts this as a message that he should become a priest, then probably it is his own desire or motive that brings about the dream. The curious thing is to note that if a tribal custom requires a dream of this sort, then it will occur.

Old and new

Some anthropologists are specializing in studying primitive people whose lives are being radically altered by contact with the outside world. In some cases, people seem to adjust quite well and incorporate Western ideas into their dream patterns, alongside the old beliefs and customs. This could provide an interesting application of dream study. It might help to show if a group was acclimatizing to the new way of life at a fundamental level or whether their adaptation was only successful to the casual outside observer. The strain of coping with a new culture, a new way of living and thinking, could be detected through changes in their dream pictures.

Many primitive peoples chose their totem or clan symbol from dream images, which in turn were usually drawn from the natural world around them – animals, birds, trees, the sun, moon and stars are often featured in this way.

Only a dream?

You may have come to the conclusion by this stage that you can read just about anything you like into a dream and interpret it in at least a dozen different ways! Of course you have to weigh up the possibilities in an image. Is it a symbol? Is it an image for something of a sexual or other nature? What did you feel about these images at the time of dreaming, and what do you feel now, thinking about it?

The chances are that there will be some overlapping between your answers, especially if you are getting close to the purpose of the dream. If you construct a 'theory' about a dream, you will immediately know inside yourself whether it is rubbish or not. But you will find that you cannot impose an idea like 'reversal' or 'displacement' on any old dream and come up with an answer. When you feel a little click in your head, or a lurch in your stomach and a voice saying 'That's it!', you will have no doubts about it. Dream interpretation only has real value if you recognize and accept the truth for yourself.

Inspiration while they slept

Through the centuries, man has used dreams in most remarkable ways to enrich his life. A wide range of achievements have been made possible through these bizarre sleep experiences. You can learn something of yourself and, if you are lucky, about the world outside.

In sleep when the mind is sifting information and the input of data is reduced, there is a greater chance of putting two and two together.

Archimedes leaping out of the bath shouting 'Eureka!' is a story everyone knows—he had suddenly worked out the secret of measuring the volume of solids by their displacement of water. In a lovely state of slumbering relaxation, with no effort from his conscious mind, he hit upon the answer to a problem which had occupied him for weeks and months.

Niehls Bohr, the famous Danish physicist, offers a more up-to-date example. When he was a student, he had an extraordinarily clear dream of a sun composed of burning gas, round which planets were spinning, attached by thin filaments. He awoke to realize that this dream image showed the structure of the atom which gave him the inspiration for further research into atomic physics. However, these flights of inspiration do not always involve such abstract scientific concepts.

Elias Howe was an American who wanted to design a really practical sewing machine. He dreamed that he was captured by savages and ordered by their king to produce a perfect sewing machine—or else! He tried and tried, but without success. His fate approached: the savages advanced raising their spears to kill him.

Suddenly Elias noticed that all the spears had eye-shaped holes in their tips. He awoke with a start and realized that the dream had uncovered the secret for which he had been searching: the thread on a machine should go through a needle hole near the tip in order to run smoothly. A small detail, but it revolutionized the design of sewing machines.

Friedrich Kekule's was probably the most well-known dream discovery. He hit upon the exact shape of the so-called 'benzene ring'—the atomic structure of the benzene molecule—with a dream image of a snake swallowing its tail. The instantaneous and accurate nature of this discovery led him to say to a group of scientists in a speech: 'Let us learn to dream, gentlemen, and then we may perhaps learn the truth'.

Thomas Edison, the inventor of the telephone, was so sure of the value of dreams that he developed the habit of snatching forty winks between hours of work and believed that a great number of his best thoughts and inventions came to him in these drowsing moments. (He was also a great believer in ESP.)

Of course, these kinds of experiences also happen to people in waking life: a flash of intuition, a sudden moment of truth is as much the way of scientific discovery as slow plodding progress. But what fascinates experts is that during a dream, which is supposed to be a jumble of images from the unconscious mind, a real insight into the workings of the world can so often be revealed.

Dreams and art

Not only in the realm of science, but in art too, dreams have their part to play.

Freud once said that it was not himself, but the poets who 'discovered the unconscious'. Throughout history, art and literature have been greatly enriched by the fantasies that have stirred in creative minds.

Shakespeare often described dreams through his characters, as a reflection of their state of mind. Lady Macbeth is a dramatic portrayal of a mind haunted by guilt: a clear image of hand-washing represents her desire to wash away her sin. In *Richard III*, the king has a tormenting dream before the battle of Bosworth—as if his unconscious is forcing him to see the tragic, drastic consequences of his lust for power. Shakespeare rightly suggests that King Richard's fear lies within himself—in the conflict between his urge for power and the pain that such destruction brings him.

Wordsworth wrote many poems as a result of dream visions—he once said that he felt he had 'lived in a dream'.

Coleridge's poem *Kubla Khan* was dream induced, although the poet also took drugs, which may have affected his imaginings.

Novelists have often found their plots and characters through dreams.

Jules Verne's *Twenty Thousand Leagues Under the Sea* certainly explores that dark underlife populated by Jungian archetypal creatures, monsters of all shapes and sizes.

Charlotte Bronte used dreams to great effect in her classic novel of childhood, *Jane Eyre*. Through the little girl's dream images, the author conveys better than any other words could express the loneliness, fear, and frustration of her life:

'A feeling as if I had a frightful nightmare, and seeing before me a terrible red glare, crossed with thick black bars. I heard voices too, speaking with a hollow sound, and as if muffled by a rush of wind or water: agitation, uncertainty, and an all-predominating sense of terror confused my faculties.' This is an authentic and vivid description of a typical childhood terror which perhaps Charlotte Brontë experienced herself, to be able to use it so well in her book.

Edvard Munch's Anxiety *captures the blank dread which must have clouded much of his own dreamworld.*

The Surrealists

After Freud's theories were first published, many artists began to dwell on the idea of the unconscious mind and thought that they too should invesigate this new way of looking at the personality. The paintings of the Surrealist movement perhaps capture the peculiar style of dreams better than any other school or generation of artists. Surrealism really began in France in the 1920s. It was defined by one of its founders, the writer André Breton, as an attempt to create art from the mind's eye, to express the real functioning of the mind 'in the absence of all control exercised by reason'. Breton wondered, as many dream theoreticians have, 'Couldn't the dream be applied to solving the fundamental questions of life?'

In capturing dream visions in paint, the Surrealists have helped people to recognize the amazing depth and richness of the unconscious mind. Their work has made people realize that there are many different kinds of 'reality' besides the one we see in during waking hours. Surrealism attempts to reach a new awareness, to lead to a better harmony between the conscious rational mind and unconscious forces. The word itself means 'over-real', a new level of consciousness, with the two levels of the mind better integrated.

Celluloid dreams

The Surrealists did not only use paintings to explore this possibility. Many of them realized the great flexibility of the motion picture to express it—notably the French writer Jean Cocteau and film directors René Clair from France and Luis Buñuel from Spain. Buñuel is still making brilliant surrealist films, superbly adapted to modern ideas. Many other film directors have played with the distinctive characteristics of dreams to convey the working of the mind very successfully. Early examples of 'dreamy' films were mostly confined to movie-fantasies, just as many dreams are pure wish-fulfilment. Women sighed over Rudolph Valentino or Clark Gable, men over Loretta Young or Jean Harlow, and the expression 'dreamboat' for handsome men is still around. But later directors began to look more deeply into the style of dreams.

The dislocation of events in dreams can be perfectly captured on film. Among the best are Alain Resnais' *Last Year in Marienbad*, Fellini's *8½* and *Juliet of the Spirits*, Antonioni's *Blow Up* and Ingmar Bergman's *Wild Strawberries*. Not just 'intellectual continentals' can do it—consider *2001: A Space Odyssey*, *Yellow Submarine*, *Barbarella* or *A Clockwork Orange*. They all have sequences that perfectly convey that mad, floating 'alternative reality' of dream experiences. Audiences have become so adjusted to this film technique now that if a person suddenly moves from one place to another—say from smiling at a child to seeing her run over, as in *Sunday, Bloody Sunday*—they know it means that the first is what is happening, while the second is what is being thought at the same split second. The essential feature of dream

Salvador Dali's 'Impressions of Africa' is a striking example of the Surrealist attempt to capture the 'other reality' of dreams.

technique in films is that so far it has only tried to imitate the way minds work during sleep. A whole new movement in the arts is trying to break down the barriers between consciously imitating and actually releasing this unconscious working of the mind through hallucinogenic drugs. The dangers behind this kind of experiment are obvious. But some people find the results so overwhelming, so startling and original however that they are prepared to take the risk. The feeling of 'breaking down the walls of the mind' was strikingly captured in the final sequence of *2001*—other examples can be seen in *Performance* or *Easy Rider*.

It's easy to see the continuing preoccupation with the 'freewheeling' processes of the mind in the 'pop' culture of today, whether the images are stimulated artificially or not. Look at the LP covers in any local record shop and you'll soon see that many have designs or photographs which draw heavily on strange juxtapositions, weird landscapes and representations of the archetypal symbols and images of all schools of dream interpretation.

Present-day research

Many psychologists believe that the brain acts as a filter, hindering our perception of 'supernatural reality', shown to some extent in dreams and the effects of hallucinogenic drugs. Present-day research is moving more and more into this realm of 'another reality'. But no one really knows the full extent of the mind's powers. Are those midnight inspirations nothing more than freak occurrences, or could dreams be used to release more knowledge? This whole area is usually termed 'psychic research' and means investigation into 'paranormal phenomena' which are not totally explicable by the present laws of science. Until fairly recently, this field of the paranormal was regarded in a dubious light, only attractive to eccentric old ladies and deluded gentlemen who liked to dabble in the occult. But now it is gaining ground as an area for serious work, and no wonder, with an overwhelming mass of well-authenticated evidence waiting to be studied.

Foreseeing the future

One of the main areas of study is precognition in dreams—those hundreds of cases where people have foreseen events during sleep. A typical incident comes from the novelist J. B. Priestley. He had a vivid dream in the 1920s of sitting in the front row of a balcony,

looking out across some dimly-seen, majestic and colourful spectacle. More than ten years later, he found himself visiting the Grand Canyon in the United States. The canyon was covered in a thick early morning mist and as it cleared, the vast, impressive Colorado landscape spread out before him. At once, Priestley recognized it as the identical place of his dream.

There are countless cases of people reading newspaper headlines in a dream announcing an earthquake or similar disaster before it occurs or at the same time, and during the First and Second World Wars mothers frequently dreamed of their sons being

Top: Buñuel's film 'The Discreet Charm of the Bourgeoisie' incorporates a common dream situation: the fear of sudden exposure. Below: the park sequence in 'Blow Up' by Antonioni brilliantly conveys the 'other sinister reality' of narrative dreams.

killed, as the event was happening.

It is possible to pass off a sizable proportion of these 'precognitive' dreams with a simple explanation. If a person wakes up for instance 'knowing' that something has gone wrong, it may be that his mind has an acutely developed sense of awareness that comes through even in sleep to give a warning in

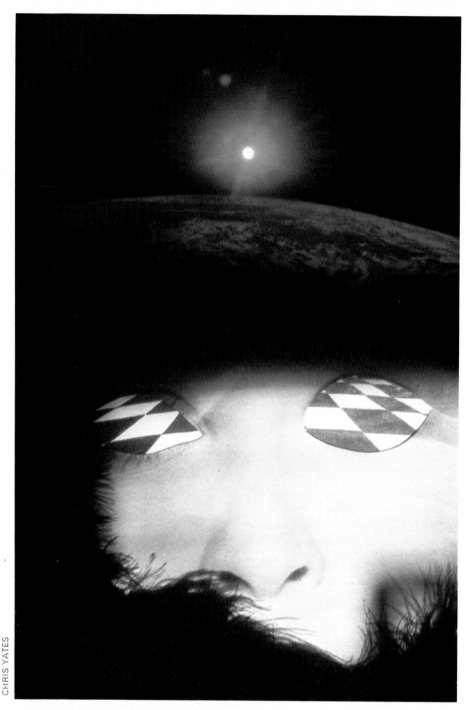

CHRIS YATES

extreme situations. This would account for those miraculous escapes from falling bombs or avalanches. Many other incidents are simply the result of worry and coincidence.

But the inexplicable dreams, foreseeing incidents that are quite beyond likelihood or visualized in such detail that they are genuinely 'psychic', pose much deeper questions. It could be that the movement of time as we know it is only one way of arranging events. Perhaps incidents in the future can 'be known' before they happen. Even more peculiar, can we know about the extreme past in great detail?

Reliving the past

Dreams about someone else's past life,

Even the most bizarre images that appear in dreams could contain a hidden meaning for the dreamer.

including names and places, have been alleged and have attracted a great deal of interest. One man could recall a previous existence as a naval gunner at the time of Napoleon and came up with such accurate details that Earl Mountbatten used the material as evidence while discussing naval history with experts. A woman called Mrs Smith seemed to recall the entire life situation of a girl who lived in 13th century Toulouse in dreams, visions and a kind of half-automatic writing. As in the case of J. B. Priestley, Mrs Smith recognized parts of her dreams on a holiday visit.

Dream communication

A theory that is being slowly accepted is that everyone has some degree of extra-sensory perception, or 'ESP'. At its simplest level, this means that you might be able to receive information from other people by a kind of invisible radio, without knowing them—and without even intending to. This would explain dreams relating incidents from the past or simultaneous events across a physical barrier, such as the problems of a relative overseas. But the real 'future' dreams are still a mystery.

Some fascinating experiments in this field have been undertaken recently by two American doctors, Montague Ullman and Stanley Krippner. They have been trying to show that in a dreaming state, people have more powers of telepathy or ESP than they do when awake. Usually these powers are associated with psychically sensitive people, but it could be that in sleep the faculty to perceive things in this way becomes much more widespread.

The experiments usually took the form of having an 'agent' who concentrated on a particular picture or idea and tried to get it across to a sleeping person, or 'subject'. The subject's dream would often incorporate the picture or idea being transmitted. The doctors learned to refine this phenomenon. Just as most ordinary dreams are concerned with people and problems, the best transmitted pictures or ideas were those dealing with these themes. So if an agent concentrated upon a picture of eating, drinking or a beautiful woman, then a male subject would be very likely to dream in a clear way of the subject matter.

How accurate are the results? In one example, the agent was looking at a painting by Monet called 'Corn Poppies'—in it a field of flowers forms the background and a woman walks across the foreground with a child. The subject's dream that night included plants, a lady 'dressed up' and a child. Now of all the things that the sleeper could have dreamed, such exact parallels with the agent's 'message' are remarkable. Multiplied by hundreds of similar tests, the results of Ullman and Krippner's experiments lead to some striking conclusions.

Nightmares could be a transmission of someone else's horrifying real-life experience. Incidents in the past might contain such powerful human emotions that they live on and get 'picked up' by another mind, even hundreds of years later. Perhaps we might even learn to develop this faculty usefully.

KIM SAYER

Leave your dreams to chance

The whole question of 'chance' may have to be re-examined in the future, if dream research continues to explore in this direction. How often have you come across some extraordinary coincidence: you dream of a friend you haven't seen in years, and the next day a letter from that same person arrives in the morning post. Normally you would dismiss this as a once-in-a-million occurrence. Now, as psychic research increases available information it seems that chance occurrences may actually be 'willed' by the unconscious.

Everyone must have experienced the terror of being chased in a nightmare: could this be the transmission of someone else's horrifying experience in life?

Interestingly, as well as exploring the unconscious mind in their paintings, the Surrealists also adopted chance methods of achieving their ends. Anything that came together on the canvas, as if by accident, might perhaps hold some unconscious meaning. The artist Paul Klee once said that his aim was to 'make chance essential'. In the light of these ideas, that is not as absurd as it sounds.

What the future holds

The real understanding of dreams is just beginning. We still have to find out how the mind selects its images. No one knows yet how memory works. The workings of so-called 'primitive' brains have to be compared with 'civilized' ones to find out if there are any real differences as well as similarities.

How much difference is there between the way children and adults dream? Is there some evolutionary progression in the hierarchy of living creatures which

governs the way they dream? What exactly is the effect of drugs and other stimulants on the working of the brain, the function of dreaming and the power of extra-sensory perception?

With all these immense questions still to be answered, the personal value of dream study has been widely accepted by experts and ordinary people alike. Some analysts even suggest that life would be greatly improved if families were to institute dream-swapping sessions, or if politicians and businessmen turned their attention to their night

Perhaps dreams will provide the key information to unlock the mind and help understand the true nature of personality.

experiences on a regular basis! Erich Fromm, a leading American psycho-analyst, has more than once advocated teaching dream interpretation in schools and colleges. So carry on dreaming, because that's where some of the most important parts of your personality are expressed and some of the richest and most worthwhile ideas have come from.